DISTANT FIRE

OTHER BOOKS BY MARTIN BELL

The Way of the Wolf
Nenshu and the Tiger
Return of the Wolf

DISTANT FIRE

MARTIN BELL

1817

Harper & Row, Publishers, San Francisco

Cambridge, New York, Philadelphia, Washington
London, Mexico City, São Paulo, Singapore, Sydney

DISTANT FIRE. Copyright © 1986 by Martin Bell. All rights reserved. Printed in the United States of America. No part of this book may be used or reproduced in any manner whatsoever without written permission except in the case of brief quotations embodied in critical articles and reviews. For information address Harper & Row, Publishers, Inc., 10 East 53rd Street, New York, NY 10022. Published simultaneously in Canada by Fitzhenry & Whiteside, Limited, Toronto.

FIRST EDITION

Library of Congress Cataloging-in-Publication Data
Bell, Martin.
  Distant fire.
  1. Meditations. I. Title.
BV4832.B395   1986   242   85-45347
ISBN 0-06-060768-8

86 87 88 89 90 HC 10 9 8 7 6 5 4 3 2 1

Contents

Preface

So now for the preface; to be sure, to be sure.

What a strange business it is when at last the unquiet writing, the struggle, has ended, finally to stop and begin at the beginning. While memory just hums right along, remembering, recalling a child, maybe four and a half years old, who is crossing alone the Straits of Mackinac on that frozen old, dead old ferryboat.

There was the real beginning: not here, not now.

Out of the north came stalking *Distant Fire,* as was its desire or necessity or something like that, making itself known then to me as it had not before, in myriad voice, ceaseless, insistent, alive.

I was not surprised.

Later, it was from the lake—from the great Lake Superior —that the unquiet words swirled out, gliding all tentative and profound, murmuring, whispering at first.

That's how I know; the book began back then with the broad-decked ferryboat riding low in the water and the child's eyes watching the land edge of lower Michigan recede, shrink, dissolve into the sad, icy waters of Mackinac. And it began with the great Lake Superior. And with Scripture, the Bible, the story of Creator God at large and at work in the world, at large and at work creating still.

Not early, God knows, did rote instruction of Scripture commence for the child—but not very late either by the usual Episcopalian standards. Though he was not listening apparently. And whatever it was that was taught in the

church school just seemed to pass from the surface of thinking without notice, without comment.

That was in another time, another life even.

Now it has turned at right angles. No longer can I separate
the living voice of the lake from all the raging, refulgent
Scripture—words so long ago hidden away, etched, within
the heart of me.

And I notice how, in the writing down of *Distant Fire,* I
have often quoted Scripture without referencing it, without
setting it off from the body of the text. I notice. But I still
believe there must not be a separation of voices—especially
after the fact; this is what I heard, this is how life comes to
me.

In truth, it was the wolf. I said, "Look, I'd rather not do
just this one thing if it's all right with you," and the wolf
waited, stood there and waited. It was as if time had ceased
and maybe now I belonged to not-time; as if the wolf were
saying, *Nothing will harm you, it will be all right.* And me, who
knew better than to worry when the wolf said not to, me just
worrying and worrying anyway, and with this strange, stubborn spirit-journey yet to be told of, chronicled, no matter
what.

When I looked back, the wolf was like the chill north
wind coming up suddenly, moaning, crying out across all of
those ancient impassive pine trees, invisible, sweeping
downward to travel then along the surface of rude, implacable Earth; I could look at the sound of it and see all the
whispering and groaning and fearful shadows—but the
north wind could not be seen, nor the great silver wolf.

Next there was nothing for me to look at except the place
where the shadow-sounds had been. So I just had to wait a
while longer (and I did and it was in the month of October)

until at last there appeared, alive and silent on the distant sky, a thin rising up of flames and of smoke.

Don't look back is what I say now.

Go ahead, disregard sequence; time isn't ultimate. Time isn't holding us down. Except apparently. And that because, for the most part, we insist on taking time to comprehend, while never comprehending at all the time that we take. But no matter.

As for *Distant Fire,* may I suggest that you open it to any page, read a few paragraphs, then look elsewhere. Or begin at the end and work backwards; the book is nonlinear, personal, provisional. It records what I can say in words about Creator God and about my own winding spirit-journey—nothing more.

Naturally, it is not finished.

Upon arrival in the upper peninsula of Michigan, the child went directly on his small and silent feet to the forest, to the lake. He made no sound at all. On his face was, I believe, an expression of intense interest which must have become surprise when the wolf appeared to him there. He looked at the wolf; they looked at each other. Then it was as if he had said suddenly to himself: *Oh, I see. I see now. Nothing else matters, means anything, except as it relates to this mysterious silver wolf. How strange.*

They were not ten feet apart, the child and the wolf—not ten feet. There was never a question in the child's mind but that the wolf was utterly special, other than himself, not a person.

Already it had begun. A spirit-journey had already begun for him who would years later watch across the cold, dying shadows of October—watching, waiting for a nimbus of fire to appear once again in the distant sky.

While at the seminary he would go to sleep in the refectory, at the supper table, quite exhausted from the stress and the harshness of theological study. He was so busy reading and attending lectures and going to chapel and writing papers that he actually forgot to be quiet, to watch, to dream.

It was a significant mistake. It had something to do with the devil, too—though not at all what he thought at the time. He would have said then that the Evil One intruded upon this world from another, quite remote domain and also that Holy God must not be held responsible for the conniving works of the devil.

He was young and he was wrong.

But now I am getting ahead of myself. Now it is like listening to a Eucharistic rite being chanted by an unknown priest in an empty church (which I have entered, apparently without knowing where I am or why I have come) and in artificial light standing quiet, thinking of how, when I was a child, the wolf first appeared to me there on the shores of the lake called Superior, and suddenly seeing the priest turn and walk from the sanctuary, beyond the choir and in the direction of a murky, unlighted transept, while I am thinking: *I know about this. I know what is going to happen next. Without stopping, the priest will go forward into the shadowland of the north transept where lingering incense breathes with waiting.* And when the howling begins, I will be thinking: *It is Yahweh who forms the light and creates every darkness. Holy and terrible is the name of the Lord.*

That is where the writing down of *Distant Fire* begins—with chanting and howling and incense and dreams. But I am indeed getting ahead of myself.

I. Shaken from the Dead

The hand of the Lord was upon me, and he brought me out by the Spirit of the Lord, and set me down in the midst of the valley; it was full of bones. And he led me round among them; and behold, there were very many upon the valley; and lo, they were very dry. And he said to me, "Son of man, can these bones live?" And I answered, "O Lord God, thou knowest." Again he said to me, "Prophesy to these bones, and say to them, O dry bones, hear the word of the Lord. Thus says the Lord God to these bones: Behold, I will cause breath to enter you, and you shall live. And I will lay sinews upon you, and will cause flesh to come upon you, and cover you with skin, and put breath in you, and you shall live; and you shall know that I am the Lord.

—EZEKIEL 37:1–6

1

Holy and terrible is the name of the Lord.

It is Yahweh who kills and brings to life; it is Yahweh who forms the light and creates every darkness. All power belongs to the Lord, the Holy One who is utterly set apart, the Unfathomable Wounder and Healer who breaks into history at will, bursting forth in furious activity among us.

God has spoken: All flesh is grass and all its beauty is like the flowers of the field—withering flesh, fading like flowers when the breath of the Lord blows suddenly upon it.

Nothing has value apart from God.

There is no infinite, intrinsic worth to the human soul. Human value is its value to God. Apart from Yahweh the nations are as nothing; they are accounted as dust on the scales; they are accounted as less than nothing and emptiness. The Word of God glides and flows across the whole creation: a creation that is perfectly sacred because the Lord God has worded it so. (And for no other reason.) To whom then will you compare me? says the Holy One.

The Lord God has spoken: I am Yahweh and there is no other. I form light and create darkness. I make weal and create woe. I am Yahweh who do all these things. Has it not been told you from the beginning? Night follows day and all who enter existence are caught in the net of the Lord; we cannot deliver ourselves from the power of the Holy. The low are raised up and the mighty are cast down. With a violent outroar the great rocks are sundered and water gushes forth upon the dry land. There is no escape from God.

And the serpent is not the devil, nor even the devil's emissary. It is Yahweh alone who stands responsible for creation. Everything that is comes from the Holy and Terrible One. Does evil befall a city unless the Lord has done it? No. Thus sin is not a serpent either. God has spoken: I am Yahweh and there is no other. You shall worship no other god, because Yahweh, whose name is Jealous, is a jealous god. And God is a devouring fire. Merciful and sinister, beneficent and dangerous, is the Maker of heaven and earth. Behold, the name of Yahweh comes from afar, burning with anger and in thick rising smoke.

2

The God of destiny is exalted above good and evil, yet is mysteriously the source of each. Without warning, Yahweh wrestles with Jacob at the Jabbok, injures and later blesses him; without apparent cause, the God of the Covenants attacks Moses and attempts to kill him; the Lord hardens the heart of Pharaoh against Moses and then smites the Egyptians because of Pharaoh's hard and impenitent heart; Yahweh drives Saul to madness and entices Ahab to destruction. We are locked in combat with God, locked in a screaming and terrifying embrace with the unfathomable, irresistible Holy One. Truth goes beyond all and every amazement: the creation is caught between God and God.

Standing present to all that is, the Creator God does not abandon or forsake or repudiate. Yahweh participates in history—snatches and uproots and blesses and restores.

But the Holy One is not any*where,* does not *exist.* And Yahweh has no *place* to be. To say that God acts in history is not to say that God intervenes or is present with us (as a finite creature might intervene or be present). Nevertheless, the Almighty does intrude, act, erupt in history. And the intrusion occurs within what we call the space-time continuum: Yahweh's bursting forth happens in various places and at different times. Surely the Lord God knows everything that needs to be known and is ever present where the Holy Presence is needed. It is enough. God is God.

God is not a person.

From the howling wasteland and from the wilderness has Yahweh called out to us. The One who rides through the desert has spoken: I am God and not man, the Holy One in your midst. Who is able to stand before Yahweh, the holy God? The gods of the people are idols, but Yahweh made the heavens. God is spirit, not flesh. The Holy One is utterly different from human beings. Neither the gods of the people nor the people may share in the glory of Yahweh. And in no sense do we partake of God's nature. There is no spark of the divine, no sliver of Creator God, in us. No fragment of Yahweh resides within human souls. The yearning of every creaturely heart is a yearning after that which is Wholly Other, Immutable, Eternal, Unsynonymous, Unapproachable.

Like a wild animal—a lion, an eagle, a wolf, a bear—Yahweh stalks the creation. Also, the One Presence manifests in lightning, thunder, wind, rain, earthquake, and fire.

Though we confess God as personal, we must never say that Yahweh Sabaoth is a person. The ways of the Holy are not our ways. And the sin of Adam is precisely the desire to be like God. A voice cries: Foolish and arrogant is every attempt to be one with the personal, animal, natural, holy Creator God.

Yahweh breathes the breath of life into dust from the ground, and the dust becomes soul. Human beings are not body and soul. Not at all. As a totality, as a living being, each of us is only soul—transitory mortal dust from the ground, brought to life for a time by the erotic breath of Almighty God. Yahweh is eternal and constant and living flame. We, who are nothing, flee to the One who created us and who remembers that we are but dust. Each of us is bound to the Giver and Enabler of life. Infinite mystery surrounds and undergirds the particles within particles. A massive halo of dark matter encircles every galaxy. On the edges of the universe there is a gleaming, invisible light that eludes discovery; it lurks and hides from every human probing; it defies science, technology, and reason. And for every answer there is another question. Human finitude cannot detect ninety percent of the mass of the universe.

And creation is continuing still.

Out of nothing, God creates. The heavens are clothed with silent, gleaming, divine brilliance. Wondrous galactic clusters spin and cosmic dust scatters through space. And in the marshes, on the mud banks of swamps, utterly new creatures are emerging: new beings, new creations never before dreamed of, are scrambling out of the bog into the sunlight. At every moment the world dies; at every moment it is being born anew. Within the shadow of unimaginable mystery, life is continuously expended and created.

Creation is not a mistake, not a cosmic accident. Ever since that first morning, Yahweh has been working toward destination, toward purpose. But God's destination is not a place, has no time; it partakes of dynamic, living expectation—a driving current of purpose that makes no sound but draws every gesture, every being, into its course. (Yahweh is not going any*where*).

The coastlands have seen and are afraid; the ends of the earth tremble.

On tiptoe a group of scientists one day entered an ancient cave and stepped into no-time where the story was unfolding in vivid, pristine earth pigments upon undisturbed rock. Note: There is no prehistoric time—only myriad images, drawings, totems, words, and sounds which witness to encounter with the Holy One. And there is no oracle to consult. No expert or authority can understand the vast miracle embodied in even a single shard of bone. We show up in an environment where others are deciding for us. And we claim ruthless questioning as our birthright. God has given each unique, unrepeatable individual the freedom to become immersed in questions to the point of drowning, to be blinded by invisible starlight, to shriek and rail against the Incomprehensible. Yahweh is not surprised or dismayed by the questioning, the anger, the doubt of finite creatures.

It is idolatry that provokes God's wrath.

In the daytime the Holy One led Israel with a cloud. All the night a pillar of fire went before them. But despite the wonders shown the people, they did not believe. And God made their days vanish like a breath and their years in terror. Yahweh made a path for destruction and anger; the Lord God did not spare them from death.

The Holy One *does* wrath, executes it: God's wrath is activity, not emotion. To say Yahweh takes responsibility for what is does not imply concurrence or endorsement or sanction. God judges and twists history toward unearthly destination. The Lord has spoken: My counsel shall stand and I will accomplish my purpose. And anyone who feels secure in wisdom and knowledge, anyone who says, "I am and there is no one besides me," shall stand under the judgment of Yahweh. The Holy One will grind into dust those who would worship many gods or give homage to the nation-state. God despises the tolerant culture. Do you not fear me? says the Lord. And shall I not avenge myself on a nation such as this? Out of the sweeping whirlwind comes a stern vision: Yahweh will scatter the bones of the ungodly, and those who fashion idols for themselves will feed on ashes. They provoke the wrath of the Lord of Hosts.

But Yahweh's love is steadfast and strong and furious.

God's passionate zeal is not like human love. It seethes and attacks and flashes. Burgeoning like a subterranean force ready to erupt into living flame, divine love moves too quickly for human understanding. Yahweh chose Israel not because it was greater or better than any other people but because Yahweh loved Israel. And the Holy One gave the people bread from heaven in abundance and delivered them from the power of the enemy. But the people forgot and worshipped other gods. Mortal minds balked at love so potent, overflowing, and perfectly faithful. We are creatures who are driven to question God, driven to examine each shredded, abandoned garment for evidence of tangible certainty. Having survived disaster and atrocity and meaningless words of assurance, the remnant of humanity rocks on a creaking front porch and spits tobacco juice. From moment to moment we decay, we drift, we die. But within the fluidity of every perception, the self still recognizes, grasps after, yearns for the Eternal Unsynonymous Other.

Language breaks under the strain of trying to speak of the Holy One. Finite syllables cannot describe the Infinite; the Living God cannot be contained within a system of beliefs or of meditative experiences. Ultimate Mystery explodes all attempts at containment. Nevertheless, the story impels us to offer imperfect, partial accounts of how we experience and know the Creator. The collection of sound and sense designated as language forms a pattern, a wheel within a wheel, spiraling somewhere between comprehension (ideas) and apprehension (experience). But what we utter is not God, nor the truth about God. Every version of the story is slanted and inappropriate and shackled to the Earth.

But the story will be told.

3

Hear, O Israel: Yahweh our God is one Yahweh.

The waters part, revealing the mercy of Almighty God, who is slow to anger, reluctant to send wrath upon the earth, and steadfast in love. All those who wander alone in the wilderness, unprotected from the pitiless sun, are strengthened by Yahweh of the Covenants.

There is no place in the world where we are lost from God.

The Creator's zeal for the well-being of the people is immutable, unchanging, unshakable. While yet remaining separate and distinct from creation, the Lord God freely chooses to act in history and is utterly affected by the peoples' plight. In mercy God does not keep the measure of our sins and iniquities; the Holy One is ever mindful of human frailty. As a father pities his children, so the Lord pities the people. Yahweh knows our frame and remembers that we are dust.

Before the mountains were brought forth, before ever were formed the heavens and the earth, God's love was operative—brooding, violent, creative. Yahweh spoke and the creation came into being; the Almighty commanded and it stood forth. Thus the erotic, creative Word of God embraced both time and eternity. By transcendence of time, as Creator and Lord of time, is God eternal. Not unrelated to time (freely choosing to ingress upon history), the Transcendent One comprehends and embraces all past, each present, every future.

And it is because Yahweh chooses to be present with us that we are buffeted and broken and consumed by divine wrath. In truth, wrath is a necessary correlate of God's love —the violent manifestation of that love in the face of human idolatry and faithlessness.

God will not let us go to hell in peace.

Behold, a young woman shall conceive and bear a son and shall call his name Emmanuel: God with us. A hand stretches out over all people, all nations; the Lord of Hosts has entered into convenant with us. The Holy One thunders and roars in judgment; the Living God comes near and then withdraws. Where shall we go to flee from Yahweh? Even darkness is not dark to God. Jonah fled to Tarshish from the presence of the Lord, but a mighty tempest arose and the waters closed in over Jonah. There is no escape from the Holy One.

We cannot ransom ourselves or buy immortality; the wise and the foolish alike must perish. Dependent, contingent, tentative creatures, we turn away from God and put our trust in graven images. We are boundlessly free to sin; individual, distinct, separate from God. But we are not dispossessed or disinherited. Every perverse breath and rebellious heartbeat is sustained by Yahweh, who watches over the captives and who ransoms the dying.

There is no security; only God's insecurity.

Our history is a holy history—the story of Yahweh Sabaoth, the One who does not keep silence, who calls out to heaven and earth, who judges and redeems and makes use of everything that is to the fulfillment of divine purpose. And there is no security, no anchor to drop in the vastness of space. There is only holy insecurity and the awesome steadfast love of the Creator—love that demands (but does not depend upon) the faithfulness of the created.

Yahweh is mindful of the covenant with Abraham and of the promise given to Isaac, which was confirmed as an everlasting covenant in each generation. The people of Israel were called from the farthest corners of the Earth to be a light to the nations and to open the eyes of the blind. They were selected to be messengers, proclaimers, witnesses, and storytellers. Yahweh chose them that they might testify to the nations of Yahweh's might and majesty and power. But the people rebelled and would not listen; they worshiped other gods and kindled the Lord's wrath against them; they became a nation among the nations. And still the Holy One did not forsake them. God has spoken: I will not violate my covenant or alter the Word that went forth from my lips. Strong is the hand of Yahweh; righteousness and justice are the foundations of the holy Word. From everlasting to everlasting does Almighty God will the salvation and fulfillment of everything that is—the whole of creation, the heavens and the earth.

If God does not save us, we shall not be saved.

Yahweh has a controversy with the people. Both judge and plaintiff, the Lord challenges and confronts: Are my ways not just? Is it not your ways that are not just? You give your mouth free rein for evil and pretend not to hear my Word.

Righteousness stretches far beyond questions of morality or immorality. It draws us into encounter with divine justice—uprightness that forgives and delivers and triumphs over evil. With grace and truth the Lord maintains a watch over all creation: a watch that is unfaltering, ongoing, ceaseless.

No act or sacrifice is required of us by the Righteous One. Only the sacrifice of giving thanks in all things. The demand is for radical God-alignment: full remembrance that the One God, who laid the foundations of the earth, is Healer and Deliverer and Judge and Destroyer. There is nothing that does not come from Yahweh, the wellspring of life and bringer of death.

4

I lift up my eyes to the hills. From whence does my help come? My help comes from the Lord, who made heaven and earth.

The recounting of holy history is the primary task of the worshiping community. Ours is a theology of recital—a theology that proclaims the mighty acts of God.

When confronting the terror of time, however, we humans tend to carve out special mythologies for ourselves. We surround our lives with images that promise to lessen discomfort, block out awareness of the inexorable progress of decay. Each of us is born, disintegrates, perishes. There is no stopping death. But, like Jonah, we flee from the one story and enshrine that which is tangible (or at least understandable), that which will serve us. Surely the family will gather together and prevent the daily trickling out of life's blood. From our children and our children's children will we derive security. If life for us seems futile and narrowing, we can live through and for the next generation. Tangible, too, are worldly riches—possessions consumed and admired without restraint. And how glorious is the nation-state, symbol of power and protection. Moreover, at the core of personal identity is the right, the privilege, to work. Degrees on the wall, nameplates, and titles are visible justifications of human endeavor. One of us is a doctor, another a clerk or a teacher or an artisan. Out of fear and panic and isolation we fashion for ourselves idols to serve as buttresses and blockades against the thunderous onslaught of Mystery.

Then it happens: At the door is a police officer who says that an automobile just struck and killed your child while she was riding her bicycle. Or your son has left home. Perhaps the business fails or your job is phased out. Perhaps you wake up one day to discover that the nation is committed to anachronistic goals. Murder follows murder and the land mourns. Palaces are built and fortifications multiply. And we who pay homage to education and profession and skill and talent find a jealous God roaring down upon us. Call upon your gods now. Command them to do your will, says Yahweh. There will be nothing solid left beneath your feet; your gods will vanish as smoke vanishes. Even religion cannot protect us from God's wrath. The Lord will drag us to the edge of the abyss and reveal the emptiness of trusting in religious practices and formulas. The god of religion is not Yahweh. Those who sow the wind shall reap the whirlwind. Yahweh falls upon idolaters like a bear robbed of her cubs. The Lord has spoken: You shall have no other gods before me. God's destruction flashes forth against the fortresses of Earth.

Electricity fills the air as terrible silver fur bristles, as the Holy One rehearses the unfaithfulness of the people in the face of covenantal love. The people demand a sign, always a sign. We forget who sustains each moment of history, each particle of the universe. We create elaborate forms of worship in order to gain security and personal integration. But there can be no transcendent integration of personality with self, society, or nature. Not yet. In truth, there is a tension at the heart of existence which makes such integration impossible.

God does not work for us; we work for God.

If we pursue religion for the sake of our own comfort, Yahweh will pour wrath upon our heads. The peace of God is not serenity. Though some measure of serenity occurs in life, it is absolutely not our birthright, nor is it a goal to be placed above uncompromising obedience to the Holy One. And religion must never become a smooth thing, a refuge, a hiding place, a haven where is heard the gentle, somnolent voice of *status quo.*

History cannot escape God's hands. But its terrors do not mean that Yahweh is unjust; the Lord's anger does not conflict with radical *agape.* Nor can history be understood as a naturalistic, cause-and-effect process; it is rather the dreadful working out of divine purpose. And the Word of God is no abstraction. Yahweh speaks through real events to real people. Therefore do we search historical occurrence for evidence of the Divine. In the saving acts of the Lord we observe that sinful human beings are used as instruments of God's love and judgment. And on occasion we catch sight of some profound, unspeakable joy.

But human beings cannot always shorten the distance between what is and what is hoped for. Unbearable pain becomes part of the given. We mourn the wasted life of a brain-damaged child, yet it is our own limitation that prevents us from penetrating the mystery and the gift of that life. No one can explain the *why* of even a blade of grass. Thus the Lord has spoken: Is it by your wisdom that the hawk soars, and spreads its wings toward the south? Where is the way to the dwelling of light, and where is the place of darkness? Scientists searching for the secret of life have discovered only lifeless atomic particles. Life has eluded them, running out through their fingers like sand.

Out of nothing, Yahweh created all that is and called the creation good.

5

There are not two principles.

Out of nothing, Yahweh created. God did not shape the world from chaos or from passive primordial clay. No confused, unorganized state of primal matter awaited the impress of divine creation.

Every dualism describes two primary, equal, and eternal principles: form and chaos. And within dualistic thought the principle of chaos limits the principle of structure or meaning. But Yahweh is not finite, not limited by any principle whatsoever. The Holy One of Israel is sovereign Lord, the sole source of all reality.

Creation was and is an utterly unique, stark, incomprehensible act of absolute origination. However, we must not equate Living God with the forces and laws of the universe; the creation did not result from an overflow of divine substance. Creation out of nothing is not pantheism. And Yahweh does not separate off, or transmit, divine light (nor does the Wholly Other One somehow permeate space, time, energy, and emergent life). God has spoken: I am the Lord and there is no other. I form light and create darkness. It was my hands that stretched out the heavens, and I commanded all their host.

Yahweh has worded all existence to be real and valuable.

Nothing in the material, dynamic world is evil at its core. The Lord God gloriously affirms the goodness of individuality, freedom, vulnerability, loneliness, finitude. Though the Earth has become a wilderness and our strength has broken in mid-course, Yahweh has not forgotten us.

In the act of creation, divine purpose began unfolding, a purpose manifested through historical event and covenant. The Lord declared a bond that would not and could not be broken, in spite of our lack of faith. No mere contract was God's promise.

In anguish we grope through the centuries—mortal, unmanageable, rebellious beings, caught by the grinding wheel of time. We carry nothing into the world, no food, no shelter, not even a name. Yahweh it is who intrudes upon us, who bursts in upon the awful anonymity of the human predicament: I have named you, says the Lord. Though you do not know me, I have named you. And I call you by that name.

The universe exists because God wills it.

Human beings were imaged by Yahweh as stewards with a special responsibility for the earthly realm. Beasts of the field, birds of the air, fish of the sea—all have been placed in our custody. That we were formed in the image of God suggests a mysterious correspondence between Yahweh and all people. The image of God also refers to humanity's free responsibility before the Creator. But specifically, it implies that the Holy One has entrusted Earth and the creatures of Earth to our care. We are called to respond to Yahweh's love with obedience and thanksgiving, though we are boundlessly free to reject the Lord's will and to walk in the ways of disruption and estrangement instead. And there has come to pass a great separation of God's unfaithful stewards from even the atmosphere that surrounds this fragile Earth. And behold, the judgment of the Lord of Hosts is upon us. We have not been vigilant. We have set ourselves up as despoilers, plunderers. Whales and eagles and seals have become fugitives from the virulent force of human greed. And now we must pay for the water we drink; the wood we get must be bought. In the dust of the streets lie the young and the old. Therefore it is time to repent of this evil and seek the Lord, that Yahweh Sabaoth might finally overcome, redeem, bring about salvation of all that is.

And salvation is fulfillment of creation, not escape from it.

At night, in the dark, in the deepest recesses of our minds, we make a decision for or against the One God. But during the day we talk about Satan, the devil, as if we were ascribing supernatural power to our world's estrangement, as if Yahweh were somehow a good force that is warring continuously with an evil force. By day sin strangles us. But at midnight something deeper gnaws at consciousness: the Holy Presence, the Origin of all creation. If faith is based on dualistic, hand-to-hand struggle between transcendent good and transcendent evil, faith will surely be shattered. All power belongs to God. Yahweh is incomprehensibly the source of both good and evil. The Holy One is ultimately responsible (able to respond) for everything that is.

Yahweh takes responsibility for evil.

That God stands responsible for evil does not mean Yahweh is the immediate and direct cause of sin. But the Holy One is able to use sin in fulfilling steadfast love; inexplicably, the Lord not only takes responsibility for evil but also uses it to bring about divine, unearthly purpose. Hear the witness of our forebear Joseph: As for you, you meant evil against me; but God meant it for good, to bring it about that many people should be kept alive.

In the shadow world between reverence and terror (the fear of God), we are free to plan, reason, decide, and act. We are distinguished from the rest of creation not in and of ourselves but because Yahweh chose us as colleagues. Human beings are not like God, however, and our freedom only dimly reflects the purposive struggle of the Creator. All analogy, all comparison, fails at the moment of encounter with Living God.

6

The knowledge of God emerges suddenly, out of the wilderness, to overtake us. It coalesces out of a windless afternoon.

Knowing God brings passionate perception of the whole inexplicable panorama of reality: good and bad, sorrow and joy. We are driven to acknowledge that Yahweh is one. The Holy One's relationship to humanity implies both faithfulness and intimacy. We are known by God in the most familiar, profound, erotic way possible. In spite of centuries of our accumulated sin, the Lord God manifests unfailing love for us. As we stumble and flounder, weighted down by evil as by a millstone, the Word announces: I will betroth you to me in faithfulness; and you shall know the Lord. But Yahweh cannot be known in abstract speculation. The Holy and Terrible One shatters into human history, penetrating all of our intellectual structures.

Meaning will not elude the person who dares to lose, to fail, to cast off from the shore of security.

Each of us is called to prophetic agony—to speak the Word, to do justice and righteousness. We are most truly ourselves when we live within God's insecurity, acknowledging Yahweh's sovereignty over creation, taking full responsibility as contingent creatures who yet must decide and act. *Future* is created out of *past* by those who live the *present*. Wherever history is unfolding, faith demands response.

In the face of God-encounter, indifference does not suffice.

Creator God is the ultimate ground for all ethical conduct: You shall be holy, for I Yahweh your God am holy. Thus, once we know the indicative, we are forced to the imperative. Anger on behalf of those who are hungry and needy and broken and desecrated is to be celebrated because it is anger on behalf of God. At the center of the universe is One who cares for us individually and corporately and who is heartbroken by our sin and who has declared a covenantal bond with us. Where there is injustice, Yahweh is the source of justice; where there is infidelity, the Lord is faithful. God has spoken: I will have pity on Not Pitied, and I will say to Not My People, you are my people.

Huddled into a faded gray shawl, wide-eyed, she stares at the barrel that is alive with fire. Cold, damp air clings to her like odorous fog. Around the barrel are gathered all the hopeless, the ragged, the hard people. An old man shoves her away when she tries to step closer to the fire. Everywhere faces are maniacal, hell-inspired. Later, in a corridor formed by bleak city walls, she walks, thinking: It is so unthinkably cold. I can't even bear the thought of sleeping on a cold sidewalk, thinking it while she is praying, praying without actual words, wishing she had a bottle of whiskey and a safe, warm bed for the night. She walks the dying city streets with her lips forming unheard syllables again and again, praying—until it happens. At a dark intersection, while she waits for traffic to clear, a cab cuts too close to the curb and throws cold, greasy water onto her legs. Then it seems as though the water has erased from her every vestige of courage. She sits down on the curb. For a long time, with head lowered, she sits there, her lips no longer moving. After that she hears another car; it stops nearby and the door clicks open. Oh God, she says inside herself, I've got to move, I've got to move right now. But her body does not remember how to respond, does not stir, even when a hand touches her shoulder. Moreover, the woman's eyes do not see who it is that places a wool blanket around her body, sets a large bundle of food on the sidewalk next to her. And in a moment the car has driven away. She sees only receding taillights as she rocks back and forth on the curb, holding fast to the thick wool blanket, forming soundless words again and again with her lips.

We are not disinherited, cut off from the Holy Presence. Yahweh has not withdrawn from creation. Surely the heart knows that the Lord's face is not hidden from us; the people are not dispossessed of the love of God. Yahweh's purpose is to heal, not to destroy.

Oh, but we have blinded ourselves and exalted the false gods of family, money, education, identity, religion—idols that are lifeless abominations in the sight of Transcendent Other. A voice cries: Will you fall down before a block of wood?

To know God is the chief duty of humankind. And rejection of this duty will bring destruction. Out of the dark and ravaged land comes the Word: Know therefore this day and lay it to your heart, that the Lord is God in heaven above and on the earth beneath; there is no other. We have heard the Word out of the midst of the fire; God's purpose has been revealed to an amazed and forgetful people. Knowledge of God is active, not passive. The call is to *act* love: cease to do evil, learn to do good, seek justice, correct oppression. Let justice roll down like waters, and righteousness like an overflowing stream. And the goal of justice is to preserve God's order. Along with righteousness, justice is the plumb line used by Yahweh to measure the iniquities of the people. But it has shown that the wall is not straight, and because it is not straight, the wall shall not stand. We have sunk into unrestrained sin, ignoring the words of the prophets, pretending not to have seen the wondrous works of Yahweh. And a people without understanding shall come to ruin. The Lord has declared: I spoke to you in your prosperity, but you said, "I will not listen." You have plowed iniquity, you have reaped injustice, you have eaten the fruit of lies. But the Righteous One acts to free us from slavery to the world. Divine wrath is not capricious or vindictive. Almighty God tears apart in order to heal; Yahweh wounds in order to bind us up; in the desert we perceive the hope of new beginnings. When life is most precarious, when our gods have failed us, when we are stripped of all worldly security, the door of infinite and eternal hope will open.

The One who rides through the desert has freed us to choose, to be consumed by the necessary task.

Let us know, let us press on to know the Lord; Yahweh's going forth is as sure as the dawn. Of a piece with knowledge is obedience—love made manifest through justice. Did not your father do justice? says the Lord. Then it was well with him. He upheld the cause of the poor and needy; then it was well. And was not this to know me? The Keeper of the Covenants desires of us steadfast love and not empty words, easy gestures. Yahweh has no use for solemn assemblies and hypocritical observances. And what does the Lord our God require of us but to fear the Lord our God, to walk in holiness, to love and serve Yahweh with all our heart and with all our soul?

We can apprehend divine sorrow, but there can be no merging of our selves with Yahweh; it is impossible to become absorbed in the Totally Other. The Holy One says *no* to mystical union, while affirming, ratifying, even demanding, intimate knowledge. We cannot become one with God any more than we can penetrate the hidden center of another human being. What *is* possible is relationship. There continues to be a peculiar, tempestuous affinity between the Lord God and humanity. Yahweh Sabaoth has laid a special claim on our lives: Before I formed you in the womb, I knew you, and before you were born, I consecrated you.

Flesh and blood cannot take credit for faith.

It is Yahweh who bestows upon us the mind to understand, the eyes to see, the ears to hear. At every moment in the history of the people, divine love is shown forth. Every choice we make is a new opportunity for Yahweh's faithfulness. It is the Lord alone who provides the means of redemption, breathes life into our dry bones.

We are made of the past; all history walks in us.

From the dawn of creation, the same chemicals and sub-atomic structures have been present in plants, animals, and people. Life feeds on life; to live is to consume the deaths of other living things. In truth, there is no way to unburden ourselves from the past. We perceive God through the eyes of history: divine wrath and love plunge into time and place and circumstance.

There is no world without weeping, no time *(chronos)* without tears. But from the mysterious deeps comes the Word of life: When the poor and needy seek water and there is none, and their tongue is parched with thirst, I the Lord will answer them, I the God of Israel will not forsake them.

7

The Lord is true God, Living God, and Everlasting Sovereign.

Incomparable in power, wisdom, and holiness, Yahweh is exalted above all. God's rule is one of fierce urgency, unexpected fury, enabling grace. Creator and creature are related in a living bond because of God's free choice; sheer Power ingresses and prowls among the people. The way of the Holy One is in whirlwind and storm, and the clouds are the dust of Yahweh's feet. Yet there is no gloom or darkness where we can hide ourselves. In the mystery of each heartbeat, we sense the Immutable One. And when life collapses and drains away, we perceive the Infinite.

It was not known why he had come to town and rented the Dedman house, which had stood empty and rotting for nearly ten years. With passive interest the town considered the man and the crumbling house and the sign that elbowed out from the front porch. A doctor of medicine he once was, and is today, as the sign says, though it seems that no one ever goes there for healing. In the daytime he sits quite alone, all calm and disheveled, on the steps of the front porch. Once on a mid-afternoon he said hello to a group of children, who thereafter scattered and ran, their voices screaming away into the mid-afternoon sun. It was his practice each day to walk to the corner market. There he would buy one or two items, taking from his pocket crumpled dollar bills, which he smoothed and straightened on the counter with trembling hands. Few townspeople ever spoke to him. For the most part they wished he would move away. Weathered by years, the wooden sign finally turned pale gray; he did not leave. Then suddenly a teenage girl from the neighborhood was missing, and the whispered talk about him who maybe was a doctor and that old house where he stayed; the talk grew louder. At midnight a crude fire bomb was thrown through the window of the old Dedman house, with the fire department arriving and putting out the fire, then leaving again, and him just sitting there all calm and disheveled on the front porch through the rest of the night. And the newspaper called the damage to his house slight— also reporting that the teenage girl had been found, when she decided not to run away after all and telephoned her mother from the bus station. Then one day in late October he was at the corner market when most of the adults were at work and the children were buying after-school candy. From behind the counter Mr. Faley, the owner of the market, raised a hand, gesturing in that instant with his whole arm, never once speaking, gasping for air like a huge fish. Terrified and motionless, the children watched as Mr. Faley lost consciousness and fell heavily to the floor. Then, all calm and disheveled, the one who maybe was a doctor put down the can he was holding and told one of the children to call an ambulance—told it without haste, without raising his voice even. He moved by means of gliding through the air, or so it seemed, so quickly did he reach Mr. Faley, who lay quite blue and dead-looking on the linoleum floor of the market. He pounded and pounded on Mr. Faley's chest. Some of the children screamed, ran away, seeing how violently he pounded. But by the time the ambulance had arrived, Mr. Faley was breathing. And after that, he who maybe was a doctor turned away from the market and the children and the cold October afternoon, walking quiet and calm, walking on up the street toward the silent old house where he stayed—the house with that time-eroded, unrelenting wooden sign.

Where human finitude leaves off, where mystery begins, there is God.

Faith proceeds from an objectivity that cannot be expressed in the language of inner experience. The story we tell is of an active God operative in the creation. Holy Presence teems and swarms and abounds. The experiences, the acts, and the words of human beings may be vehicles of revelation—but human personality and experience are never the focus. In the king of Assyria, Yahweh found an instrument to wield against Israel and Syria. And the scriptural witness is clear—it was not the Assyrians who defeated the people, but God acting through the infidel armies: Ah, Assyria, the rod of my anger, the staff of my fury!

Creator, Victor, Judge—Yahweh has covenanted to be always with the creation.

Covenant relationship, based on God's steadfast love for us, never alters course. There is an immense, eternal sameness to Yahweh, whose faithfulness stretches the limits of our imagination. Yet Inescapable Presence responds to a pulsating, chaotic world differently at different times. Yahweh will not forget or forsake human creatures, but divine response to those creatures will not everywhere and always be the same. Within the unfolding of holy history, Emmanuel (God with us) is variously manifested as blessing, destruction, and Living Presence. Even so, God, who is totally separate from the dynamic creation, does not grow or change or become. Yahweh transcends, surpasses, soars above all nature and all time, while using both nature and time to accomplish unearthly purpose.

It is perilous to be the vehicle of God.

We are called to do the Lord's will—though we are a sinful people living in the midst of a sinful people. Unable to resist evil, we must rely on the Holy One to provide the means of redemption. And Yahweh our Sovereign is from of old, working salvation in the midst of creation. A voice cries: The Lord lives; blessed by Yahweh, my rock and my salvation.

God alone is Sovereign. None other holds sway over creation. All earthly power depends upon, proceeds from, the Holy One. And this sovereignty extends to our minds and hearts; our thoughts are not concealed from the Creator, who sustains each moment of life. The Lord has spoken: My eyes are upon all their ways; they are not hidden from me, nor is their iniquity concealed from my eyes. The high and lofty One that inhabits eternity, whose name is Holy, indwells the realm of finitude and limitation.

Only with awe and dread do we dare state who God is or what attributes Yahweh possesses. Righteousness, love, jealousy, holiness, wrath, and eternality can only be inferred from historical event. Men and women of faith have pointed to certain occurrences within the chronological order and have called these: God-events. Our witness to the Holy One does not spring from theoretical speculation. It arises out of raw life-struggle—day-after-day events, dilemmas, episodes, calamities, miracles. Though utterly transcendent, Yahweh conquers and destroys illusion, scatters injustice. The sovereignty of Yahweh bears witness to the realization that God will not tolerate our trusting to any political order. Every election, decree, negotiation depends finally on the Unsynonymous. And the people will know that righteousness and justice are the foundation of God's throne; steadfast love and faithfulness go before the Lord. Our eyes have seen the glory of the Lord of Hosts.

To confess God is to tell a story and then expand upon its meaning: A wandering Aramaean was my father; and he went down into Egypt and sojourned there, few in number; and there he became a nation, great, mighty, and populous. And the Egyptians treated us harshly, and afflicted us, and laid upon us hard bondage. Then we cried to Yahweh the God of our fathers, and the Lord heard our voice, and saw our affliction, our toil, and our oppression; and the Lord brought us out of Egypt with a mighty hand and an outstretched arm, with great terror, with signs and wonders;

and Yahweh brought us into this place and gave us this land, a land flowing with milk and honey.

We need to say the words aloud; the story must be told again and again.

Black smoke rises from the middle of a field, its origin obscured by tall weeds and scrub pines. Perhaps the gray wood of an abandoned shed has burst spontaneously into flame. Or perhaps there is a presence, as yet unseen, tending a deliberate burning of underbrush. What burns, and at whose hand? It is tempting to cut across the field and approach the thick cloud of smoke. But the afternoon heat discourages. And there are ten miles more to walk before reaching town. Time floats somewhere between the overturned earth and the empty, motionless sky.

Moses said to God, "If I come to the people of Israel and say to them, 'The God of your fathers has sent me to you,' and they ask me, 'What is the name of this God?' what shall I say to them?" God said to Moses, "I AM WHO I AM." The name reveals and does not reveal. Immediacy and urgency are conveyed: God will be God; Moses' commission is to lead the people out of Egypt. Moreover, within the name dwells power, reality, blessing. It signifies the presence of God, the holiness. And the name is impenetrable; Yahweh *means* the Unsynonymous, Eternal, Infinite, Wholly Other. The divine name *is* relationship, God's response to historical circumstance.

As living souls (without any separation between spirit and flesh), we rehearse the fact of our finitude and limitation. We call upon the name of God for strength and courage, knowing that Yahweh, the One who gives life, also demands death. Spirit journey is life journey, passage from dust to dust, the brief flicker of time during which flesh is enlivened by the breath of God.

Now in the hollowed-out earth, whitened bones are spliced together, sinews reknit; skin covers flesh. A voice speaks; and from the high ground many winds assault the valley until at last the whole people stand and cry with a loud shout: Blessed be the Lord forever!

II. Fierce Shepherd

> Then he took his staff in his hand, and chose five smooth stones from the brook, and put them in his shepherd's bag, in his wallet; his sling was in his hand, and he drew near to the Philistine.
>
> —1 SAMUEL 17:40

1

Is not my word like fire, says the Lord, and like a hammer that breaks the rock in pieces?

Divine revelation is fraught with Mystery. Even in self-disclosure, Yahweh remains the hidden God. The encounter belongs to the Holy One; human beings can neither initiate nor control it. Through mighty and gracious acts, Creator God hastens to meet us, addressing us within the context of the physical world. We cannot bring about revelation; no technique or method can be devised, no experiment conducted, that will uncover the Infinite. God is the Absolute Subject who is always confronting. At a certain where and a particular when, human beings behold divine self-disclosure—a promise of meaning beyond monotony and pervasive fear. And whereas life appears to be tragic, absurd, even pointless to many, nevertheless, the Holy One freely chooses to act, to *do* revelation—the Word of God. From the wilderness comes both judgment and hope. The east wind, the wind of the Lord, shall come from the wilderness and the fountains shall dry up. And yet in the wilderness also is the covenant given, and the valley becomes a door of hope because Yahweh's purpose is not to destroy.

History is our environment, the air we breathe.

The secret things belong to God, but the things that are revealed belong to us and to our children forever. Behind the ongoing mystery of life and death is the Sustainer of life; behind the grinding wheel of history is the Lord, who stands utterly responsible; behind the moment of crisis is the Creator, who redeems. Animal-like, Yahweh roars from the desert; in the air is an awesome electricity from the bristling of the fur of God. In truth, we have been exiled within our own land. And the wrath of the Holy and Terrible One is felt throughout all the earth. Yahweh is like an enemy, scattering the people in the wind. Yet a voice cries: In the wilderness prepare the way of the Lord, make straight in the desert a highway for our God. Every valley shall be lifted up, and every mountain and hill be made low.

Our eyes have seen the great works of Yahweh, but human beings cannot know the full depths of Ultimate Mystery. When the encounter comes, we are cautioned that it is holy ground on which we stand. We are consigned to think and speak of the One Presence in a way that is not fully possible. Familiar words stretch to express the extraordinary; there is no sacred or revealed language. To say that the Lord is ineffable (beyond human describing) is to deny the historical witness. Nor are creatures limited to saying of Yahweh only what Yahweh is not: not this, not that. But human speech is primarily finite in its reference, and language cannot express God in the same way it expresses tangible, worldly reality. When words are applied to that which transcends space and time, they become figurative, symbolic, analogical. Further, in every attempt to speak about God, all sorts of apparent contradictions appear— language becomes paradoxical.

God is both subject and object of revelation.

The strong hand of the Lord seizes us, impels us into the thick of history. The Word of God is not confined to spoken or written language. Much more is meant: act, event, thing, happening. God raised up a child to go before the Philistine. The child left his father's sheep in another's care and said, "Send me. I have killed both lions and bears." Then with one smooth stone David felled Goliath, the Philistine of Gath. The Holy One does not impart abstract truth, nor is the Word a matter of inner experience. In our struggle with the daily and the catastrophic, we have no protection, no armor. Only five smooth stones in a shepherd's bag. The crowd jeers and mocks. Giant corporations and bureaucratic school systems disdain us: Are we dogs that you attack us with sticks? But the scattered, dispersed, trammeled people of God know that the battle is the Lord's and all power proceeds from Yahweh Sabaoth.

In the prophet, God marries a person with history.

Without warning, any one of us may decide to become a sign, to proclaim Yahweh's Word in such a manner as to startle, surprise, bring sudden awareness. Prophets don't care what the secular state has to say; they hold up a mirror that the people might see themselves and be appalled by their own iniquity. Prophets stand before the councils of multinational corporations and proclaim that the wrath of God has been revealed through the actions of the Middle Eastern nations. The platform from which Yahweh speaks is public: I do not speak in secret, in a land of darkness, says the Lord. And history rushes down upon us, a tidal wave of incontrovertible events; we cannot retrace our steps. Each historical event is singular, unique, unrepeatable. But our lives are not determined, decided, by fate. We are up against the Totally Other, the Lord of Hosts. Yahweh's Word is very near—it is manifested in event and prophetic announcement.

The Word of God will not be silenced.

The story is irreplaceable and ongoing. One walked naked and barefoot as a portent against Egypt and Ethiopia; another took a wife of harlotry as a sign of the Lord's faithfulness to the covenant; yet another sat in a seat forbidden to her and refused to move. All these announced the Word while forces of opposition gathered in fury, determined to erase their witness. But the prophets point beyond themselves, beyond events, to the Unapproachable One. Thus the Word of God becomes *act* which determines history.

No person or thing is worthy in itself to represent the Ultimate. But neither is any part of creation excluded from being used by Wholly Other as a means of revelation. (When the people returned from exile in Babylonia, it was through the agency of God's chosen instrument, Cyrus, the infidel king of Persia.) Revelation precipitates our identifying with even the most unlikely of God's people. And holy history advances in disguise, wearing the mask of the preceding scene. Through historical events we come to know God; we rely on revelation for knowledge of the Holy One.

There is nothing that does not reflect the power of God.

A passenger descends from the train. Underfoot, rough concrete sidewalks rub away at the worn leather soles of his shoes. Men and women pass by. Their faces look blank, as if the passenger has no substance, no reality. "What's the use, kid?" says the tired voice inside his mind. "You'll never make it—too young, no experience. You'll get slaughtered." Then he takes his staff in his hand and chooses five smooth stones from the brook and puts them in his shepherd's bag, in his wallet; his sling is in his hand, and he draws near to the Philistine.

Every prophet speaks with the cadence of the holy. God's Word is hurled at us like a stone. In revelation there is always a call to decision: Choose today whom you shall serve. Yahweh is not concerned with imparting factual information. The Lord God provokes relationship and response. And the Word leads finite creatures into strange, unfamiliar territory where they are cut off from not-God —the secure, the idolatrous. Yahweh has spoken: From this time forth, I make you hear new things, hidden things that you have not known. They are created now, not long ago.

2

Blinded by questions, aching with unnamed longing, we grasp after Ultimate Mystery.

And the people asked Moses, "Have you led us out of Egypt only for the purpose of killing this whole assembly with hunger? Would that we had died by the hand of the Lord in the land of Egypt." So Moses, shepherd of the people of God, said, "Take your complaints to Yahweh—what am

I that you complain to me? Your murmurings are not against me, but against the Lord."

The Holy One stands outside the realm of human existence but freely chooses to enter into relationship with the creation. Yahweh's self-disclosure comes to us through historical events that human beings identify as the action of God. This, then, is revelation: event, witnesses, and faith-proclamation. Faith-proclamations are vivid, dramatic, often poetic statements about what God has done. Language about Yahweh includes both immediate response and subsequent theological reflection. The ongoing work of the people is to retell the story in order that it may be heard and understood by each new generation. Revelation is received by faith (which is itself God-given). And faith always involves making decisions in the face of uncertainty. God seeks out those who reach beyond their grasp—those who dream on behalf of the whole creation.

The richness of language used for proclamation testifies to complex and radical God experience. Analogical, symbolic, metaphorical language allows us to describe the encounter: Yahweh breathes life into dust, thunders in the heavens, flashes forth lightning; judgment and destruction come through animal-like power; the Almighty is betrothed to Israel as to a bride. Concrete, even anthropomorphic, ways of speaking about Yahweh are necessary to the language of faith. Faith-language affirms a special correspondence between God and the world (an analogy of being). Without such correspondence there would be no way to talk about God at all.

In strength and in weakness did David appear before the Lord. As anointed king of Israel, he captured the impenetrable fortress of Jerusalem and established a mighty nation. But David also knew the depths of human anguish. He stood before Yahweh as a broken, sinful man. Like David, we are in constant conflict with the Unfathomable One we serve; we are stretched to the very limit of our abilities in that peculiar service.

Those who survive the battle with Yahweh are the remnant.

We must do the impossible; we must survive. Because in our time there is profound devaluation of both God and humanity. The culture seeks to subsume all faith unto itself, to homogenize and soften the ancient witness. We live under house arrest, afraid to walk familiar streets at night. The old, the mentally ill, the handicapped are isolated within institutions, and we are deprived of their gifts. Society has dug a network of tunnels in the thick darkness of the unknown. We have honeycombed the world with *verifiable facts.* Some deny that the idea of God has any meaning whatsoever; they reject language that refers to transcendent reality. Many insist that statements about what we know are meaningful only if they can be verified or falsified in some way. The torch of factuality is brandished in order to push the darkness back. And a new tunnel has been constructed for the purpose of separating faith from rationality. A voice cries: It is idolatrous to ascribe such authority to human reason.

Yahweh does not understand (stand under, support) the delimiting of cognitive meaning in this fashion: I created every rationality, says the Holy One. Shall I flee because reason is shown to be of the created order, finite? No. Human beings cannot even verify the creation by means of rationality; how then shall they verify the Transcendent? And why has knowledge been limited to the verifiable? God has spoken: Let all the earth fear the Lord. Let all the inhabitants of the world stand in awe of Yahweh!

The day is coming when the earth shall see utter discontinuity, the end of time within time, a new age that transforms the old. Time after time has Yahweh exhibited forbearance. The Lord watches over the sojourners, lifts up those who are bowed down. But the people put their trust in economic, political, and military strength, instead of relying on the Holy One; thus the nations decline. But we who have been swallowed up by the secular state still look with hope to the fulfillment of Yahweh's Word. History squeezes down from the many to the few, from all people to Noah, to Abraham and Sarah.

Until we have recognized God as the enemy, we have not yet learned to pray.

And it came to pass that Jerusalem, city of David, was conquered and the Temple destroyed; the nation was dispersed, the leaders deported to Babylonia. The Lord gave full vent to his wrath; Yahweh poured out hot anger, kindling a fire in Zion that consumed its foundations. And those who remained near the ruins of Jerusalem were like orphans, bereft of their heritage. Nevertheless, the people continued to recall the steadfast love of Yahweh. And by the waters of Babylon there arose a hope, a profound expectation, for one who was yet to come. To the people in exile came a hope:

that there would issue forth a shoot from the stump of Jesse upon whom the Spirit of the Lord would rest: the spirit of wisdom and understanding, the spirit of counsel and might, the spirit of knowledge and the fear of Yahweh.

With a dying crescendo, the people lamented in their exile: How long, O Lord? Will you hide yourself for ever? How long will your wrath burn like fire?

As the shepherd rescues from the mouth of the lion two legs or a piece of an ear, so shall a remnant of the people be rescued. Yahweh will gather the remnant of Israel and set them together like sheep in a fold. God has spoken: I will leave in the midst of you a people humble and lowly. They shall seek refuge in the name of the Lord. And the remnant will no more lean on political powers or sociological studies or on the god of manifest destiny; they will lean on Yahweh the Deliverer, who will restore them. A voice cries: Then I went down to the potter's house, and there he was working at his wheel. And the vessel he was making of clay was spoiled in the potter's hand, and he reworked it into another vessel, as it seemed good to the potter to do.

During one turning of the earth long ago, someone some-where mixed together certain substances to produce colors, which were carefully applied to the wall of a cave. Experi-ence was translated symbolically into story. It was a matter of life and death: a composite picture of all time since cre-ation and of God's not-time before life ever ran under the skin.

We know not whence we came into this dying life.

But time is running out for us: the creatures of God and of midnight rambling, the children of the morning, on the horizon dawning like an awful and irrevocable hoping against hope. Time is running against us, while sin abounds and abounds with real death and real evil stalking about, naked as the world and mean as hell.

3

Primarily, sin is not a moral term.

And evil is not eternal. Nor is reality in and of itself deplorable. We are not strangers in a strange land. The Earth is sacred as we are sacred; it is our home and our responsibility. Yet each person is born into a state of separation that is inherited just as surely as Noah's grandchildren inherited the flood. No guilt can be extracted or squeezed from this primordial state—only mystery. Original sin is as undeserved as God's redemption. Before we are conscious of any such concept, sin dominates every relationship, every perception of the world.

We show up into a condition of conflict.

To be born is to be separated. When the umbilical cord is cut, life takes on edges and angles. What was smoothly flowing becomes sharp, cold, other. Plunged into chronological order, the child reaches out with alarm: the wilderness leans inward, and solitude becomes total.

But human existence is no more essentially evil than it is divine. We are an integral part of a creation that has been worded by Yahweh to be *good* (meaningful, purposed, destined). Fulfillment of life does not consist in escaping the human condition, avoiding pain and suffering.

We are immersed in nature. And the entire world is creature—given life and sustained by the One God. But also, the world is distorted, alienated, estranged. Feelings of emptiness and hopelessness abound; we are separated. And guilt arises when original estrangement is compounded by personal acts. Personal sin yields guilt. We choose disobedience instead of righteousness, rebellion against God instead of justice. The essence of sin is always betrayal of divine love.

Personal sin is the opposite of faith.

The act that compounds original sin ought not to be set over against virtue or goodness. Rather than immorality, the issue is idolatry. In our pride and delusion we rebel against the sovereignty of God and rely on the strength of living beings. And who can say, "I have made my heart clean; I am pure from my sin"? Each of us is bent and twisted and empty and divided. A brooding, desperate humanity widens the chasm that separates us from the totality of the environment. Human greed builds nuclear reactors on soft, loamy soil, dumps toxic waste into uncorrupted rivers and streams. Therefore prophets address the regulatory agencies that allow industrial plants to belch chemical pollutants into the atmosphere: You have made this land a horror. The birds of the air and the beasts have fled and are gone. Woe to those who build a town with blood and found a city on iniquity.

Prepare for yourselves an exile's baggage.

Consumerism is molded into brightly colored paper and plastic idols. Woe to those who say to plastic things, Awake; to a stone, Arise! Can these give revelation? The advertisers purvey illusion, and we believe the lies. Yet our ears are closed to the anguished cries of the planet; the trees can no longer breathe; fish lie dead on the beaches; human strength is hunger-bitten, and calamity is ready for our stumbling. Irreplaceable petroleum, complex mixture of hydrocarbons formed in the Earth's upper strata, is burning out of control.

To the nations who seek power over Earth, prophets declare the judgment of the Lord: Because you have plundered many nations, all the remnants of the peoples shall plunder you.

The homeless seek hope in the sun, following the myth of progress; terrorists arise in every land; those who have food to eat and fuel to heat their homes complain of needing more distance from one another.

Year after year, the burden of sin grows heavier. Spent and crushed, longing for life, we cry out: There is no health in our bones, no soundness in our flesh. Sin pervades even our thinking. Rationality is clouded, confused, limited. Our hearts are deceitful and desperately corrupt, loving evil more than good.

But at the heart of sin, behind every particular image or example, is estrangement, disruption, separation. The power of evil goes far beyond every shameful immorality of the world; its strength is derived from tragic, all-pervasive alienation. Human beings are alienated from themselves, from others, from the creation, and from God. And there is no way to avoid sin; it is a condition that cannot be solved by efforts of the will. Moreover, we are dismayed to discover that good deeds cannot reverse estrangement: we are in a state of sin from birth, guilty of faithlessness unto death.

Alienation is inescapable.

No person can enter the life of another, know another's tragedies, joys, terrors. Each of us lives in a separate universe. It is *given* that we cannot fully understand each other. It is *not given* that we must do violence to one another. Yet the land is full of blood, the cities full of injustice. There are those who would make gods of themselves, persuading the people to drink poison until everywhere around them the ground is savage with death. And the King of Tyre was cast down because he said in his pride, "I am a god." And the King of Babylon said in his heart, "I will ascend to heaven; above the stars of God I will set my throne." Therefore was he cast down also.

Sooner or later, our idols will be shattered and the pieces snatched away by the wind. And healing will come from Yahweh, who is strength and refuge but also terror and demand. It is repentance the Lord seeks: a faithful heart, obedience through love, rejection of idolatry.

And Yahweh humbled you and let you hunger and fed you with manna, which you did not know, nor did your fathers know; that Yahweh might make you know that man does not live by bread alone.

We shape parables and allegories and hymns to become vessels for the Word. Familiar sayings are infused with new meaning; the remnant issues forth in new life. God chooses what is foolish to shame the wise. The small and unpowerful shall bring down the mighty. And people who once felt they were no people shall realize they are the people of God. Yahweh has spoken: Behold, I send my messenger to prepare the way before me, and the one whom you seek will suddenly come to his temple; the messenger of the covenant in whom you delight, behold, he is coming, says the Lord of Hosts. But who can endure the day of his coming, and who can stand when he appears?

4

In despair we hope against hope. Apathy alone is hopeless. After every attempt to find meaning within ourselves has failed and irresistible compulsions continue to enslave us—there on the edge of despair, we perceive the Holy Presence.

Humanity is not utterly depraved. We did not fall from goodness into corruption. And God is with us even as we raise a fist and curse God.

Human mortality does not constitute punishment for rebellion (though we use physical death as a symbol for divine judgment on sin). We were not created immortal; death is a natural aspect of existence that becomes terrible only through sin. Out of finitude we shriek an indictment against suffering and death and unknowing. We blame Yahweh for our estrangement. We say that the way of the

Lord is not just, when it is our own way that is not just. It is our eyes that are closed, our ears that refuse to hear. We conceive of ourselves as prisoners of the past. But in truth, it is the past that enables the present. Somewhere in the dust, in the sand, are the bones of people unknown to us except by their work; these individuals struggled and questioned and breathed so that we might live.

We are neither the guests nor the victims of God.

Evil is operative solely in the temporal realm; it has no metaphysical, no other-worldly power. Satan is personified evil: a symbol for human compounding of sin wherein the whole is greater than the sum of its parts. As a totality, sin seems to have metaphysical dimension. But it does not. The devil reigns as symbol for the principalities and powers of *this* world—the dark alienation embedded within creation. But Satan's power is not like unto Yahweh's. And although at times we get to thinking that the devil must have conquered God, nothing could be further from the truth. Evil bears various names—the Adversary, Satan, Devil, Belial—and stands antithetical to God. But Satan is merely a way of describing the immense evil of the world, nothing more. Satan is not an angel who fell, or an evil god. From Yahweh comes all. God sent the evil spirit upon Saul and later put lies in the mouths of false prophets. The desire to concentrate myriad forces of evil in one personal image is human. It grows out of our uneasiness when encountering the Holy One.

Demons, too, are symbolic, metaphorical creatures who represent the dark powers of this world—though here the evil represented is usually more individual than societal.

When human beings are ensnared by illusion, by delusion, by idolatry, they are said to be demon-possessed. Yet the Holy One stands present to alienation, takes responsibility for evil, and makes use of sin unto the fulfillment of divine purpose. The powers that are hostile to Yahweh have no transcendent reality; they are projections of our own finite, rebellious condition.

A strange by-product of creation is evil, which Yahweh stands responsible for yet absolutely will not abide.

The Almighty is at work in history, calling the world away from evil, altering creation through redemptive action. To humanity Yahweh has given the freedom to be other than divine. We are free to reject the Holy One. But sin does not exempt us from responsibility. In the end we must acknowledge that we are not God and take our place in the great sweep of holy history. The Lord has spoken: Bring forth the people who are blind, yet have eyes, who are deaf, yet have ears! Let all the nations gather together, and let the peoples assemble. Remember not the former things, nor consider the things of old. Behold, I am doing a new thing; now it springs forth, do you not perceive it? I will make a way in the wilderness and rivers in the desert.

Hell belongs only to this world.

On the analogy of personal relationship, God is separate from us, allows freedom, but seeks our response in love. And to say that all people are sinners is not to deny the differences among us. Trembling before the mystery that is yet to be, we confess that evil is a fact, a reality, not an illusion. But it is an existential fact. And we look forward to the redemption of everything that is, when the glory of the Lord shall be revealed and all flesh shall see it together.

5

The ancient witness possesses unique status. Testimonies contained therein are primary; they provide a canon (measuring stick) by which all subsequent revelation is tested. Yahweh's self-disclosure is always tied to, informed by, the faith-proclamation of those who have gone before. Contemporary witness depends on the story of Yahweh's action in Moses, Deborah, David, Isaiah—though what is revealed in the Exodus event or in the Babylonian exiles is not universal religious truth. What is revealed is the Holy One. Moreover, Yahweh seeks out humanity—we do not discover or create God.

The message of the ancient witness is unique. Israel was chosen to be the elect of Yahweh, a light to the nations. Israel was chosen out of the limitless depths of mystery— not because of innate morality, sensitivity, or faithfulness, but solely because God loved Israel. Abraham laughed when Yahweh announced that Sarah would bear children in her old age; Moses and Jonah and Jeremiah each tried to avoid Yahweh's commission; David caused Bathsheba's husband to be killed in battle. In the midst of faithlessness and reluctance and immorality was this people chosen to be a sign unto all people.

Theology is in constant dialogue with the ancient witness.

The ancient witness discerned a pattern of divine action in history for both judgment and salvation. The prophets were sociopolitical analysts in God's employ; during and after Israel's time of exile, as a sense of Yahweh's unfolding purpose deepened, many looked forward to a climax within history, a time of fulfillment when the Holy One would raise up a new Israel. The prophets told forth God as impending historical crisis.

Already what was going to happen had begun to happen.

Had not Moses said: The Lord your God will raise up a prophet like me from among you? And Jeremiah's witness was thus: Behold, the days are coming, says the Lord, when I will make a new covenant with the House of Israel and the House of Judah not like the covenant which I made with their fathers when I took them by the hand to bring them out of the land of Egypt, my covenant which they broke, though I was their husband, says the Lord. But this is the covenant which I will make with the House of Israel after those days, says the Lord: I will put my law within them, and I will write it upon their hearts; and I will be their God, and they shall be my people.

Isaiah had spoken of the faithful remnant, and Ezekiel had proclaimed a resurrected Israel. And from outside/within the fabric of the chosen people was emerging a nameless, indomitable Something; all of history was emptying itself toward a perfectly new moment. From the earliest sea of life through the rise and decline of a mysterious Middle Eastern people had that Something been making its way. And now —now the world was on the verge of being turned inside out. History clattered and drummed through the vacuum of space: first came Israel's call, then the deliverance from Egypt, Torah law, entrance into the Promised Land, the Davidic kingdom, two Babylonian exiles, the rebuilding of Jerusalem, Hasmonean rule, Roman oppression. Thus did holy history jostle and career through the wasteland of time. And all the while, Something was approaching.

But you, O Bethlehem, from you shall come forth for me one who is to be ruler in Israel, whose origin is from of old, from ancient days. And he shall feed his flock in the strength of the Lord, in the majesty of the name of the Lord his God.

Messiah would be wise and righteous and powerful, God's anointed, yet fully human. The one expected would resemble a known quantity: Moses the leader, Elijah the prophet, David the political-military victor—especially David, the perfect king, powerful enough to capture Jerusalem, yet deeply committed to Yahweh. Comfort, comfort my people, says the Lord God. Speak tenderly to Jerusalem and cry to her that her warfare is ended, that her iniquity is pardoned. And it shall come to pass that I will pour out my Spirit on all flesh: For to you a child is born, a son is given; and the government will be on his shoulders, and his name will be called Wonderful Counselor, Mighty God, Everlasting Father, Prince of Peace.

The biblical witness follows no system. Throughout, there is a certain marvelous, lively inconsistency. The people of the covenant are not philosophers. They are women and men of faith, passionate, driven, grappling with Yahweh Sabaoth. Their commission is to live in the world, to communicate divine revelation in the historical arena by means of formulating images, pictures, words, that point beyond the created order to Unsynonymous Redeemer God. Theology grows out of philosophy but partakes of passionate involvement. And whereas the philosopher may choose a stance of relative detachment, the theologian must be committed, both proclaiming and interpreting the faith.

Theology is not necessary for salvation, but it is necessary to the vitality of the believing community.

Thus the prophet speaks: The Lord has anointed me to bring good tidings to the afflicted, to proclaim liberty to the captives, to proclaim the year of the Lord's favor and the day of vengeance of our God. Whatever was to happen was beginning to happen. And the Spirit of the Lord was hard upon the prophets. They felt the trembling of the universe, sensed an oncoming Something—central, implied, though not yet revealed. Moving toward the climax of God's self-disclosure, the whole creation faltered. A voice is heard in Ramah, lamentation and bitter weeping. Rachel is weeping for her children; she refuses to be comforted for her children, because they are not. And Israel, wretched, broken, singled out by Yahweh, was filled with fear and a sense of helplessness. Isolated islands of consciousness inside bags of skin, separate, lonely beings confronting what was perceived as hostile judgment upon faithlessness, the people closed their ears to the prophets.

6

The dilemma of finitude is couched in paradox. Every part of our nature is corrupted by sin. We are fallen in the sense that, like Adam, we want to be God. Human beings become hypnotized by temptations to power or control or self-determination. Yet psychology cannot bring reconciliation, and wealth cannot restore community. The created order stands in need of a salvation that no earthly power can shape. Within history, Yahweh's intervention is the substance and subject matter of concern; all else is marginal. And a mantle has been cast upon us, though we try to avoid the immediacy of the Word (And Elijah passed by and cast his mantle upon Elisha who said, 'Let me kiss my father and my mother, and I will follow you,' and Elijah said, 'Go back again, for what have I done to you?'); we are called upon to answer impossible questions while living impossible lives. And we are sent to testify *now* to those who are dying—not tomorrow or next month. The engagement between God and humanity is a fantastic, vital, cosmic dialogue filled with conflict, frustration, and joy.

The believer lives simultaneously in faith and in doubt.

We are not one with God; therefore, we experience separation from the Holy One as a given of existence. Yahweh is Creator and Sustainer but Yahweh is not present always and everywhere as world-soul. God is not the environment. To believe means to hold on firmly, to trust tenaciously in the Lord. But acceptance of doctrine is not faith. If all doctrines and theological concerns are seen as a wheel, then faith is the indispensable hub. Nevertheless, whenever we attempt to think or speak about God, we find ourselves making use of theological insight. In other words, we seek to understand as best we can.

Faith that is blind is not faith.

To communicate belief involves explaining, unfolding what is meant by original proclamation. The brimming, boiling-over enthusiasm (filled with God) of the faithful

community gives rise to a story. And the community inter-
prets what the story meant then, means now, will mean in
the future. Thus a richness of testimony emerges: proclamation, teaching, social comment, hymns, drama, poetry.
Preaching proclaims the ancient witness and also begins an
interpretation process. Individual believers are sent into
the world to be instructed and to instruct, to hear the story
and to announce the Word of God. The task of theologizing is always a matter of life and death. There is a dynamic, combustible quality to the story.

You can't just rely on someone else's faith.

Some put their trust in commerce, and some put their trust
in weaponry, but we will put our trust in the name of the
Lord. Faith in Yahweh cannot be disguised as part of a
sanctified culture.

Come, let us return to the Lord; for Yahweh has torn in
order to heal, stricken in order to bind up. Original sin
describes an aspect of the human condition; it does not
represent a tragic defect that is transmitted from generation
to generation, a defect that could have been avoided. We do
not carry sin like a disease. Nor does sin exempt anyone
from responsibility. God is God no matter how we feel
about it. Thus sin brings judgment; judgment demands repentance; and repentance opens the way to redemption. And
Something is advancing toward the earthly realm, turning
back the outermost edges of the universe, doubling creation
in on itself. Have you not known? Have you not heard? The
Lord is the everlasting God, the Creator of the ends of the
earth. The Holy One does not faint or grow weary; Yahweh's understanding is unsearchable.

In political ferment the prophets saw the coming of liberation. The servant nation was thinned out by catastrophe into a tenuous line which had already begun to quaver and vibrate with God-identification. The people were thrust out of a narrow passageway into a new wilderness. Israel had been refined by the fire of affliction. Time was crowding and huddling and piling up like snow against a picket fence. Divine purpose was reaching out, touching the earth with expectation. Then came the Word of the Lord: For a brief moment I forsook you, but with great compassion I will gather you. In overflowing wrath for a moment I hid my face from you, but with everlasting love I will have compassion on you.

Yahweh was recreating the holy community.

First the Assyrians, then the Babylonians destroyed cities, looted temples, transported people into bondage. Later, through Yahweh's instrument, Cyrus of Persia, the people of Israel returned to Jerusalem. Thus the Lord has spoken: Cyrus is my shepherd, and he shall fulfill my purpose. But all the while, history was drawing nearer and nearer to realization of Something as yet to be, while the people dreamed of a future based on the past, a hope rooted in prior understanding. But the prophets knew. The lucid ones sensed Something utterly unique, felt history connecting with that which had never been. The prophets knew: And I will pour out on the house of David and the inhabitants of Jerusalem a spirit of compassion and supplication, so that when they look on him whom they have pierced, they shall mourn for him, as one mourns for an only child, and weep bitterly over him, as one weeps over a firstborn. Lo, your king comes to you; triumphant and victorious is he, humble and riding on an ass, on a colt the foal of an ass. His dominion shall be from sea to sea, and from the river to the ends of the earth.

What was going to happen was already beginning to happen. And from outside/within the fabric of the chosen people, Something was about to be born.

A voice cries: And the wolf shall dwell with the lamb, and the leopard shall lie down with the kid, and the calf and the lion and the fatling together, and a little child shall lead them. Self-determination shall give way to repentance; smug recital of religious platitudes shall yield to astonishment and awe. Through grace will come right relationship with God. And the people have seen the great chasm between humanity and the Holy One. But now at last they shall see the gulf bridged. The Lord has spoken: Behold, my servant, whom I uphold, my chosen, in whom my soul delights: I have put my Spirit upon him, he will bring forth justice to the nations.

7

Time was collapsing under the weight of divine crisis.

Opportunity had been heralded, and fulfillment was waiting at the borders of the universe. Along the continuum of events, a certain buckling could be perceived: purpose was speeding toward the heart of a small Judean village. And while the people searched the eastern horizon for earthly vindication, a hurricane was bearing down upon them from the west. A terrible knowledge without words was growing: the expected messiah had not come, but the unexpected (an

abrupt tearing of the fabric of reality) was close at hand.
Though only a very few people were infected with the dark
secret, it held them with magnetic force. Measured time was
being subsumed into fulfillment, breaking through, colliding
with the ordinary turning of the Earth.

Time-space is given meaning by its content. Yes, and all
seasons, all moments, are in Yahweh's hands. The final arbi-
ter in history is Yahweh Sabaoth. Days and months and
years constitute divinely interrupted sequence. Thus, the
people waited, preparing for God's ingression—but they
knew neither the place nor the hour.

No-time was about to collide with Earth time.

The crisis, the collision, was imminent. Circumstances
were swirling toward an awful, terrifying coincidence of
chronology and eternity. Thus says the Lord: In a time of
favor I have answered you; in a day of salvation I have
helped you. And the undercurrent of measured time moved
silently along the bottom of the ocean. It had no expectation
of being interrupted. Prophets and monastics heard the first
distant rumblings as the structure of reality began to break
apart. Where there was smoothness, there arose craggy
cliffs; where there had been calm, there came shocking dislo-
cation of human presuppositions. The current of chronological time was permanently diverted. A fierce Shepherd God
took the creation by ambush as no-time converged with
daily time and fulfillment thundered on into eternal night.

The servant nation had been refined and reduced to One.

Human history was unnavigable, out of control, im-
measurably displaced. Yahweh's action did more than re-

store, went far beyond vindication. The shocking, contradic-
tory God held onto creation like a priceless pearl. We were
about to be freed from enslavement to the ordinary, to death
and the fear of death. Place and moment were selected. Then
from the house and the lineage of David came a new origin,
a birth completely unlike any other. Bitterness melted away;
virulence evaporated in the harsh, swift astonishment of
colliding dimensions. Not a sound was heard. And one
lonely star burned overbright, like a candle in the darkness,
in reverence to what could not happen. The entire universe
watched and waited and held its breath while time was
fractured, split, severed. I myself will be the Shepherd of my
sheep, says the Lord God.

Yahweh seized the opportunity, the right moment, for the
fulfillment of divine purpose. History is not a collection of
happenings, but a series of times-with-content sent by the
Holy One. *Now,* in Bethlehem, city of David, was born the
ultimate incarnation of Time by which the chronological
order would finally be overcome. Yet they slept in their beds
—the people of Israel, the Roman oppressors, even the
prophets. Because what was awaited had not come. And
what God purposed was so new, so unexpected, that the
glory of it was unseen except by a very few. The Unsynonymous became flesh. Creation was reordered. Genesis began
again, reversed itself, as one bright star stood present on
behalf of all galaxies, all worlds. And angels appeared to a
group of isolated shepherds who were keeping watch over
their flocks by night. The time is even now fulfilled, said the
Unexpected One; glory to God in the highest, the angels
proclaimed; let us travel to Bethlehem, said the shepherds.

But the shepherds did not understand what they perceived. No one could yet understand. Because what had

begun, what had miraculously transpired, could only be partially apprehended, not understood. A perfectly new moment had arrived. An utterly dissimilar occurrence had come to pass, a hope beyond imagining, a burnished promise—the new covenant. It happened in Bethlehem of Judea. On a night when almost no one noticed, a light shined in the darkness.

God's love is arbitrary, irrational, unmerited.

III. All the Distant Voices

Then I looked, and I heard around the throne and the living creatures
and the elders the voice of many angels, numbering myriads of myriads
and thousands of thousands, saying with a loud voice, "Worthy is the
Lamb who was slain, to receive power and wealth and wisdom and
might and honor and glory and blessing!" And I heard every creature
in heaven and on earth and under the earth and in the sea, and all
therein, saying, "To him who sits upon the throne and to the Lamb be
blessing and honor and glory and might for ever and ever!"

—REVELATION 5:11–13

1

It was not a gentle birth.

All human suffering and grief accompanied holy Mary
into that rude and strange birthing room. Thus was the child
wrapped in swaddling clothes, surrounded already by the
smell of death, with on him even in his manger bed the
shadow of a cross.

The one who was expected did not come. Instead there
arrived in the Judean darkness, beneath that brilliant and
immobile star, the enfleshment of Affirmation, fully human/
fully God, bridging the unbridgeable chasm of none-such
between creature and Creator. Soon, human cruelty would
seek to smother the child; the principalities and powers of
this obscene world would discern the jarring intrusion of the
Infinite and shriek with outrage. Yes, time had ripened and
burst forth. The Word no longer stalked the world; the
Word was in the world ready to do hand-to-hand combat
with evil and death and meaninglessness. Like a huge boul-

der, the Christ event bore down upon the world's rank, inflexible power with the same force that at the dawn of time had pressured and shaken and shaken and pressured until something was created.

There was never a time that did not know Christ.

But no previous moment had witnessed this incarnation, the enfleshment of God. The preexistent, tumultuous power manifested in Jesus Christ touched, tore at, broke open the heart of creation. God was in Christ, reconciling the world unto divine passion. But the unity of Yahweh was not broken. What happened was that the One God attacked creation, rearranging time and space. Like water erupting from beneath parched earth, the Holy One attacked. It was not a gentle birth. Divine love and wrath came to perfect fruition in the child. What had never been absent from us—the Holy Presence who delivered the people out of Egypt and who judged their sinfulness—now dwelt among us. Emmanuel (God with us) had become incarnate: the Christ. And Yahweh thus revealed was one; the same Yahweh—only different.

Creation trembled.

The man of sorrows had entered the world. Out of the remnant of Israel came the one who would lay down his life and by whose sacrifice all history would be unified, healed.

And all the while, the forces of evil were working through Herod, King of Judea. When he sensed the cosmic trembling, Herod sought to kill the Intruder, slaughtering innocent children in his frenzy. But the Christ child was already in

Egypt (Out of Egypt I have called my son), and Herod did not, could not, find him. Yahweh's incessant hammering at the foundations of human sin and apathy was taking new shape: an implacable, redemptive acting and choosing across impossible boundaries. What had begun was now unfolding and increasing and extending and sprawling. Yet only a few were given the vision with which to perceive the ultimate reaching-out of God. One voice cried: Lord, now lettest thou thy servant depart in peace, according to thy word; for mine eyes have seen thy salvation which thou hast prepared in the presence of all peoples, a light for revelation to the Gentiles, and for glory to thy people Israel.

Also in those days came John the Baptist, preaching in the wilderness of Judea; behold, I will send you Elijah the prophet, said the Lord.

But even John did not understand how Yahweh was bending and twisting human expectation.

John's call was for repentance (turning around) in preparation for the coming of God's kingdom. It was a significant proclamation, but even so it missed the mark. There was not a single person who expected or imagined the truth. Yahweh had caught hold of the creation in a startling, unique way. Most startling was the awful fact that what was actually happening *could not be happening.* The world was being turned inside out while everything continued to look the same. Or nearly the same. John the Baptist strode on the mudbanks of the River Jordan, heralding the advent of the Kingdom of God, a kingdom that would replace Rome, a messiah who would overthrow the Roman Empire. To the oppressive Roman state, what John preached was treason. Drawing closer and closer to his own death, John shouted to the crowds: I baptize you with water for repentance, but he who is coming after me is mightier than I, whose sandals I am not worthy to carry; he will baptize you with the Holy Spirit and with fire.

What did you go out into the wilderness to behold? A reed shaken by the wind? Why then did you go out? To see a man clothed in soft raiment? Behold, those who wear soft raiment are in kings' houses. Why then did you go out? To see a prophet? Yes, I tell you, and more than a prophet. This is he of whom it is written, "Behold, I send my messenger before thy face, who shall prepare thy way before thee."

The divine tumult, which had brooded and waited and watched since before creation, was now incarnate. But John did not know. In the process, chronological time had been shattered like a watch that breaks upon sudden impact. But John was not aware of this displacement. Animal-like, personal, utterly transcendent, Yahweh had taken time by the throat and transformed chronology into high time, the *eternal now* of divine fulfillment. Silently, the Kingdom of God was born. Human expectation went unfulfilled; unearthly purpose did not. That which always was and had no beginning was first *looked upon* in Bethlehem. The people who walked in darkness had seen a great light: A child's cry was emitted from a rude stable while a lonely star blinked in response. And the whole cosmos shifted. The Unsynonymous was now fully human; the Totally Other took on mortality. And wise men from the east traveled to Bethlehem, wondering, diligently searching, half-blinded by starlight and dreams. The magi saw a king and rejoiced; Herod feared a king and spilled the blood of innocents.

And to no one was the fullness of time revealed. Not yet.

A hurricane, inexorable and violent, was moving rapidly toward its destination. Dark, foreboding tragedy kept constant company with Jesus. And the Source of all was ever present, obscuring human vision, waiting with infinite patience for violent, chaotic, sudden time-fullness. It was Christ who shattered the idols of the people in the wilderness, and Christ who pronounced judgment by the mouths of the prophets. None other than Christ held the plumb line as a measure of Israel's iniquity. There was never a time, a history, without Christ, though at destination Bethlehem, Jesus the Christ became living soul (flesh and blood) out of impossibility—as could never be, but was and is, and is to be. It is enough. God is God.

2

It was Yahweh, incarnate in a squalling, helpless, threatened child, who entered the world. For no human reason, without human motivation, the Unsynonymous One became flesh. By all rights, the absolute tension of no-time colliding with all-time should have destroyed creation. But Yahweh's purpose was not to destroy. The Holy One intended redemption, new being, restoration—though history appeared to be proceeding along the same halting course; except to a few visionaries who did not fully comprehend, but sensed after, interpreted, read the uneasy signs of the times. And these prophetic ones began to proclaim the advent of Something awesome and dangerous and ultimate. John cried: Even now the ax is laid to the root of the trees; every tree therefore that does not bear good fruit is cast down and thrown into the fire. Repent, for the kingdom of God is at hand. Bear fruit that befits repentance, and do not presume to say to yourselves, "We have Abraham as our father"; for I tell you, God is able from these stones to raise up children to Abraham.

But to what shall I compare this generation? It is like children sitting in the market places and calling to their playmates, "We piped to you, and you did not dance; we wailed, and you did not mourn."

The Remnant One, born of Mary, stayed behind at the Temple in Jerusalem when he was twelve years old. The Unexpected One, who refused to fulfill human expectation, sat among the teachers, listening, asking of them, questioning—a solitary, uncanny child, climbing and climbing to ever more treacherous heights.

The devil said: If you are the Son of God, command this stone to become bread. The devil said: To you I will give all worldly authority and glory—for it has been delivered to me, and I give it to whom I will. The devil said: If you are the Son of God, throw yourself down from the pinnacle of Jerusalem's temple; for it is written, "God will give angels charge of you to guard you." But there was no safety for Jesus. And the Word he proclaimed was everywhere the Word of holy insecurity and risk.

The strangeness of it was the infinite possibility.

A steadily mounting stress was working its way through the life of the child-become-man. The shepherds left their sheep unattended in response to that stress; the wise men paid homage in the midst of it; Anna and Simeon were impelled to give thanks to God; Herod and all the forces of the world flashed with rage as they were caught up, crushed, hemmed in, by increasing, unearthly stress. The tightening noose caught and killed John the Baptist, who, while in prison, sent messengers asking: Are you the one? Is the kingdom of God upon us? Has the announcement been fulfilled? John sent messengers. And the Word that came back to John shook the foundations of the earth (as indeed that Word had shaken every human generation): Look around! What do you see? Is not Yahweh drawing humanity into the embrace of holy combat and uncompromising love?

The Son of God questioned every answer.

It was left to John to discern the first signs of Yahweh's intrusion. The fullness of revelation was yet to come. Incarnation was not an answer. It changed human perception of death and life and God—to the end of reestablishing a right relationship with the Holy One. But there is only one covenant; God's love never changes. What came about was a new understanding of the one covenant. The dynamic, surging Christ event from of old, which had manifested throughout history, now commingled with human blood and skin and bones in the person of Jesus of Nazareth.

Think not that I have come to abolish the law and the prophets; I have come not to abolish them but to fulfill them.

And over a period of some thirty turnings of the earth, a new light was shed on the old covenant, a new telling of the story unfolded, as confrontation of God with humankind was squeezed into one unthinkably small hunk of geographic space. No wonder evil skulked and seethed and plotted to kill the Stranger! Never before had the world known covenant enfleshed. Demons fled from Jesus—tried

to escape the power of life. And those who considered themselves faithful were angered by the One who questioned
their comfortable, controllable god; Yahweh would no
longer tolerate trivialization. Those who sought to tame the
God of the Covenants were reviled and rebuked by the
Christ. Judgment had been spoken by the prophets, the
historical mediators of Yahweh's Word. But now the Word
was enfleshed; holy history had culminated.

*Go and tell John what you hear and see: The blind receive their sight and
the lame walk, lepers are cleansed and the deaf hear and the dead are
raised up, and the poor have good news preached to them.*

All that had been separated, deformed, broken apart was
being made whole through Christ. And the awful mystery
of incarnation was reversing any human claim to understanding of the how or the when or the what of Creator God.
In truth, we have always traveled in a tunnel of unknowing
—from the earliest days of survival by a river on a continent
as yet unnamed. Yahweh gave us dominion over a world we
did not understand. But the scribes and the Pharisees
claimed to know; the Zealots and the Sadducees had fashioned answers for themselves. Many there were who
claimed knowledge of God while compounding the atrocity
and unspeakable suffering of life. They were wrong.

*O Jerusalem, Jerusalem, killing the prophets and stoning those who are
sent to you!*

Layer upon layer of skulls and jawbones and fragments
of fossilized life appear along a remote shoreline. One perfectly preserved skeleton of a child is yielded up by ancient
earth while a serpent winds through the parched grass. And
nearby are remains of creatures no human being has ever
seen: dinosaurs who lived, then disappeared, sixty-five mil-

lion years ago. Behold, the Mystery revealed to paleontologists who work in the hot, stinging winds of Africa is the same Mystery revealed on the banks of the River Jordan. No amount of human exploration can conquer the unknown; no astronomer can unlock the universe. Yahweh reaches into history with violent love and snaps human presuppositions like so many twigs.

God sanctified the struggle of the child who sank into marshland a million years ago, sanctified it by means of the One who took all life unto himself. That which *was* from before the beginning of time now became vulnerable human dust. He was called Jesus (Yahweh will save), a new Joshua who would lead the people of God into a new land, a land overflowing with promise and fulfillment. With the advent of Jesus, the Totally Other walked among us. Yahweh of the Covenants did more than intervene: the Unsynonymous became ensnarled in the human condition. The Word was the same Word, but the revelation was utterly unique, once-for-all.

Humanity looked upon the face of the Mystery—and survived.

3

They searched in the desert and in the Temple and in the skies for the first fruits of the kingdom; some looked for direct intervention by Yahweh, others for a human agent. And indeed Jesus proclaimed, as John had, that the kingdom was at hand. But soon this announcement began to shock and frighten and anger. Moreover, Jesus refused to be quantified or categorized; the Word could not be controlled. In

Nazareth the people tried to enclose Jesus in a furious embrace, but he disappeared from their midst—only to reappear elsewhere. The hungry wanted food; the sick gathered to be healed; the Pharisees demanded answers.

Jesus claimed a new authority beyond even that of David.

Before Abraham was, I am.

David ate of the Bread of the Presence when he and his men were starving; Jesus' disciples plucked and ate grain on the Sabbath as a sign that Yahweh's law is not an end in itself. The Healer of all does not intend us to ignore the needs of others. And on the Sabbath, in violation of Deuteronomic law, Jesus restored to wholeness a man with a withered hand while the Pharisees looked on, horrified. And Jesus stared at them in anger, grieved at their hardness of heart.

Is it lawful on the Sabbath to do good or to do harm, to save life or to kill?

The Pharisees were silent. But Jesus broke their silence. A rushing wind shook the foundations of human security; an uncanny power echoed among them. With terrific urgency, the Man for Others taught and healed and preached the imminent arrival of Yahweh's kingdom. Christ, the power of God and the wisdom of God, opened the eyes of the blind, acted upon, shattered, the lives of disciples and skeptics and detractors. Healings and miracles heralded the messianic age; the prophecies of Isaiah, Amos, Hosea, Zechariah were fulfilled. Many were comforted, others were reproached.

An evil and adulterous generation seeks for a sign; but no sign shall be given to it except the sign of the prophet Jonah.

And the terrible power of God was revealed through shock and surprise. Jesus railed against the arrogance of the Pharisees, then berated his own disciples for their lack of understanding. The Incarnate One could never be predicted. He jarred and startled people into repentance; the works of Jesus were a savage, free-wheeling foretaste of the kingdom —works to which the proper response was not awe or wonder but radical God-alignment. Thus, the cities where many miracles took place were upbraided because they did not repent. And far from repenting, the scribes were scandalized when Jesus presumed to forgive the sins of a paralytic.

Why do you question thus in your hearts? Which is easier to say to the paralytic, "Your sins are forgiven," or to say, "Rise, take up your bed and walk"?

The healings and miracles were intended to unsettle, to disturb the complacency of the people. And Jesus Christ used and twisted messianic expectation to God's purpose. Now the cup of prophecy was filled to overflowing. Jesus laid claim to being messiah—but with him, all former images tore like silk. He was every messiah and no messiah. Ancient prophecy was freighted with new significance: A young woman shall conceive and bear a son and shall call his name Emmanuel. In Bethlehem of Judea, the Christ event extended Isaiah's vision. Yahweh roared and sprang upon the people with unbridled power; the Word became flesh to stir life force within those who were dead.

The Christ crowded human pride into a corner.

To those who came in search of a formula for eternal life, Jesus answered: Be like God, be perfect, do the law. And when a rich man claimed to have done the law, Jesus told him he must also sell everything that he had; this the man could not do. And so was the rich man's illusion of earning eternal life broken, scattered in the wind, lost forever. The Son of God cast out the demons of delusion and pride and caution and security. Jesus could not be manipulated to human ends. Those who awaited calm encountered a storm; those who prayed for a storm were becalmed.

4

Jesus was not, is not, essential humanity.

And he is not the perfect representation of humanity made in the image of God. There is no unity between Yahweh and creation. We have not fallen away from perfection; we were created as mortal beings, given purpose and meaning by God. Jesus is not different from us simply as a matter of degree—more faithful, more complete. Something utterly disjunctive from humanity became enfleshed at Bethlehem (fully human/fully Yahweh). Nor is the Jesus Christ merely an incarnation of God's plan or intention. Our faith is not rooted in the shallow topsoil of living, holy example.

Conversely, the attitudes, actions, and decisions of Jesus were not, are not, those of God. The enfleshment of the Holy One is far more complicated than that; incarnation absolutely may not be understood as Yahweh wrapped in an outer garment of flesh. To be explicit: the One who bore our griefs and carried our sorrows experienced real oppression and real affliction. The Incarnate One was battered and bruised and tortured; he was crucified until dead and then buried by the world, the flesh, and the devil. And that suffering is an indispensable key to the revelation of God in Christ.

It was not a perfect human being who shouted down the hypocrites or refused to see his family or cursed the fig tree.

But even so, what had already happened had yet to happen.

5

In the desert, Jesus fasted forty days and forty nights. Elijah, too, fasted forty days on his journey to the mountain of God. And Jesus, after his baptism, was led by the Spirit into the wilderness. There, the principalities and powers of this world besieged him just as they had assailed the people during the forty years of wandering following their baptism in the Red Sea. The Christ came out of nowhere and began preaching repentance: The time is fulfilled; the kingdom of God is at hand. Chronology has ended, and God is bringing about divine purpose. This is not the season for excuses or for dodging the Word!

Follow me, and leave the dead to bury their own dead.

In the wilderness Jesus consciously prepared for the sacrifice of the Suffering Servant. He turned away from, rejected, the heroic image. A hero would feed starving people with bread, or lead them in a military campaign, or at least display the supernatural powers associated with an apocalyptic messiah. The Remnant One renounced heroic consciousness. Yes, there was a time in Israel's history when heroes (called judges) gave the people life, but that time had passed. Under David the kingdom flourished. Now, political answers would not free the people and could even further enslave them. The Word that came growling out of the desert said *No* to a political, economic, cultural messiah. The wilderness agony foreshadowed Christ's Passion; it heightened in the man Jesus a peculiar form of messianic consciousness (Suffering Servant) which was diametrically opposed to the heroic consciousness of apocalyptic expectation. And out of the desert of devil-confrontation burst an intentional, frightening, irrevocable ministry.

The entire sweep of holy history was compressed into what followed. In Jesus Christ, prophetic insight had been infused with vehement, passionate life force. An immense human yearning that was born near the waters of Babylon now appeared by the shores of the Sea of Galilee. A dangerous, unsleeping journey had begun. Jesus committed himself to the Cross the moment he turned away from temptation in the desert. His was a thoroughly intentional, profoundly angry advance through many towns, across the wilderness, into hill country, and beyond.

Christ incarnate was the fulfillment of centuries, eons, of divine faithfulness.

But the people were bewildered, even dismayed, by what they saw and heard. And by what they did not see and hear. Whereas the healings and miracles (signs and wonders) pointed to a dawning messianic age, nevertheless, Jesus often cautioned those who had been healed to keep secret what had happened, to tell no one what their eyes had seen and their ears had heard. In part, at least, Jesus hid from the people. Yet there could be no doubt as to what was being claimed. By the first century, certain passages from the prophetic writings had been given high messianic significance. And the man from Nazareth invariably patterned his ministry in dialogue with these crucial passages.

After John was arrested, Jesus emerged from the long shadows of the desert, traveling from gleaming white sands into the wooded hills of Galilee, where he taught as one with messianic authority. And a man who had an unclean spirit cried out, "What have you to do with us, Jesus of Nazareth? Have you come to destroy us? I know who you are, the Holy One of God." And Jesus healed many who were sick and cast out many demons; and he would not permit the demons to speak further, because they knew him.

The time was not right for disclosure.

The people pressed in upon Jesus, some out of need, others in wrath. Danger followed him. And death followed too, listening as the ruthless preaching echoed and echoed away in the cold desert night. To the Roman-controlled government Jesus represented insurrection; the Romans perceived him as arousing the common people against the political order of Caesar. Subjugated Jewish authorities feared the widespread consequences of any rebellion. Yet Jesus refused to lead the crowds; he turned his back on every opportunity to incite the people and, instead, gathered ever-increasing tribulation unto himself. It was a hurricane that was headed toward Jerusalem. At least that. But at the eye of the hurricane was the Suffering Servant. And, except to certain elite messianist groups, the mysterious Suffering Servant figure seemed to be just the opposite of messiah. Some who were waiting and fasting and praying for the arrival of a new age had already suggested possible (though radical) correspondence between messiah imagery and the Isaian Servant. But no one had yet woven all of the threads into a single strand. Now, therefore, the Incarnate One touched the heart of every expectation with the fire of God; John purified with water, Jesus with harsh rebuke and shocking grace.

The Remnant One *was* the Word of God—at once fulfilling messianic prophecy and rejecting any and all orthodox interpretation. Few there were who suspected his real purpose, mission, destination. Even the sons of Zebedee asked to receive the chief places in what they believed would be the Davidic kingdom.

You do not know what you are asking. Are you able to drink the cup that I drink, or to be baptized with the baptism with which I am baptized?

But that which was to come was not the Davidic kingdom, although Jesus was the Son of David and soon would be a fugitive as David had been. It was the primacy of Yahweh that consumed the Man for Others. Nothing could distract him from preaching Yahweh and Yahweh's kingdom. However, as the forces of opposition became more focused and the people refused to relinquish traditional expectation, Jesus suddenly turned in an irreversible direction; he self-consciously chose to offer himself as a ransom for humanity.

6

The Messiah spoke in parables, knowing he was being watched by his enemies.

He referred to himself as Son of Man—a human being, one who belongs utterly to this world but who has been called to unique mission by Yahweh. The language and imagery of the created order were beginning to break under divine stress. Prophecies that pointed to disparate messianic traditions were being churned and mixed and twisted. Jesus was not simply a prophet; he was the fulfillment of all prophecy. In him faithfulness was completed. And occasionally his searing impatience with human pride flared out of control. Yet Jesus recognized the faith of many; and he sought out the lost, the despised, the abused. Before long the Lord's Anointed would drink the cup of suffering to the dregs. But the people did not understand. Even his disciples expected a different messiah. Religious and secular authorities continued to watch and to wait and to design various snares and traps. Everyone was uneasy. In truth, the man from Nazareth would soon become a living nightmare to the principalities and powers of this world; he would outrage them and violate their deepest understanding of reality.

Yet on behalf of the Syro-Phoenician woman, the publican who could not raise his eyes to heaven, the uncomprehending multitudes, the tax collectors, the Pharisees, and the Roman oppressors, Jesus continued to move through the countryside preaching Yahweh and repentance and the imminent arrival of Yahweh's kingdom. And his words pierced the fabric of history like an arrow.

Blessed are your eyes, for they see, and your ears, for they hear. Truly, I say to you, many longed to see what you see, and did not see it, and to hear what you hear, and did not hear it.

Yahweh our God is one Yahweh! The Holy One is not tied to images of the past. When Israel became a nation among the nations, the Babylonians (God's instrument) scattered them and destroyed the temple. When the people put their trust in a political messiah who was to be ruler of a restored nation, Yahweh entered history and smashed the messiah idol. The Living God was the Savior who raised up deliverers from among the people: tribal leaders, generals, kings. Yahweh has spoken: I am the Lord and besides me there is no savior. All redemption comes from the Wholly Other. But in Christ, humanity beheld Redeemer God. (For to you is born this day in the city of David a Savior who is Christ the Lord.) Hear the Word of God: I will betroth you to me forever; I will betroth you to me in righteousness and in justice, in steadfast love and in mercy. I will betroth you to me in faithfulness; and you shall know the Lord.

Intricate, fragile galaxies bore silent witness to Yahweh's desire, yearning, reaching out, at incarnation.

The God of the Old Testament is the God of the New Testament. Thus, Christians cannot escape the jaws of Yahweh—furious, thundering, overturning tables in every temple that has ever been, exploding, creating even now out of nothing, creating. And Jesus' teachings are not the gospel, the Word of grace; they are kingdom sayings, calls to repentance, fulfillments of prophecy. The gospel is the *being* of Christ (not Being itself), the enfleshment and sacrifice of God Almighty, the incarnation of covenant. At last, human beings, deeply corrupt and ensnared by sin, saw in Jesus the full implications of the one covenant. Radical love of Creator for creature shined fierce and brilliant in the darkness. There is one God. There is one covenant. It is enough.

And grace is Yahweh's covenant-love, which neither acknowledges nor allows for any barrier whatsoever. God's redemptive purpose encompasses all people, every universe.

The undeserved gift of grace is not withheld from even the darkest corners of creation. There is no distinction. All have sinned and fallen short of the glory of God. Nor can humanity somehow earn grace or buy the Lord's favor. Yahweh is under no obligation to us except the freely chosen obligation expressed in the one covenant. The nature of grace underwent no change from ancient times to the time of Jesus. It was humanity's vision that changed. Everything (from alpha to omega) has always been enabled and sustained by grace freely given; there is no way to invoke it or to initiate its power.

For I came to call not the righteous, but sinners.

From the inner depths, the Word of life was brought forth.

7

In Galilee, as time moved toward Crisis, the sayings of Messiah-not-messiah became more and more alarming.

I have come to set a man against his father, and a daughter against her mother, and a daughter-in-law against her mother-in-law; and a man's foes will be those of his own household.

The Christ-demand transcended family loyalty, requiring full allegiance to Yahweh, insisting on radical commitment. A pungent fear swept over the disciples. That which had begun in the desert now was moving toward the agony of divine completion. And Jesus had compassion on the harassed and helpless crowds who followed him over the hillsides like sheep without a shepherd; these were they who fulfilled the prophecy of Isaiah: You shall indeed hear but never understand, and you shall indeed see but never perceive. Jesus had compassion on the desperate and frightened multitudes. But as for the Pharisees, who attributed his power to the prince of demons, he was without compassion; he condemned their hardness of heart, their blaspheming of the Spirit. Death accompanied Jesus as he taught and preached and even when he withdrew to pray.

The ministry of the Incarnate One was a paradoxical proclamation of the primacy of God. The Living God, he declared, soon would reveal all that had been hidden, obscured, from creaturely sight. Jesus confronted and prophesied and healed. And Herod Antipas was kept informed by spies who reported that some were saying this was Elijah, while others called Jesus a prophet like the prophets of old. But, in his madness, Herod said, "John, whom I beheaded, has been raised." And indeed, the perplexing, unidirectional preaching of the man from Nazareth was disturbingly similar to John's. With sluggish fascination, Herod continued to gather information about the Stranger, not yet suspecting that Jesus had already begun to bear the Cross that he would carry all the way to Golgotha.

And no one puts a piece of unshrunk cloth on an old garment, for the patch tears away from the garment and a worse tear is made. Neither is new wine put into old wineskins; if it is, the skins burst, and the wine is spilled, and the skins are destroyed; but new wine is put into fresh wineskins, and so both are preserved.

And Jesus challenged the twelve with the question of his own identity. Twelve disciples, representing the twelve tribes of Israel, alternating between faith and doubt, chosen to carry forward a mission on behalf of all humanity—it was these who had to decide. Simon Peter dared to speak: You are God's Anointed, the Son of David, the Messiah. The words were spoken at Caesarea Philippi, in a region out of which flows one of the sources of the Jordan River. And ironically, the baptism with which the disciples would be baptized was initiated by that confession: You are Messiah, Yahweh's holy agent for the ushering in of the kingdom. Yet when Jesus began to divulge the implications of suffering and death that would accompany the intentional forcing of time into Crisis, Peter refused to listen, could not bear to hear of it, would not believe.

That which was yet to happen remained hidden. The disciples followed what they did not comprehend because their hopes were based on traditional imagery—in spite of what they had seen and what they had heard. And Jesus impatiently rebuked Peter, more to fulfill prophecy than in real anger against the simplicity of understanding that filled the being of his fisherman disciple. Broken, sinful, confused people were being called as witnesses to Something utterly new, unnamed, not fully revealed.

Whoever would save his life will lose it, and whoever loses his life for my sake will find it.

Jesus claimed to be Son of God in the same way that the ancient witness set forth Israel as the firstborn of Yahweh. Jesus announced it. And prophecy after prophecy was fulfilled by the Remnant One who perceived the way of messiah to be identical with that of the Suffering Servant. But once John the Baptist had been executed, it became increasingly difficult to elude the treacherous minions of the devil, the hypocritical scribes and Pharisees, the spies of Herod Antipas, and the dissidents among his own followers. Only the Son of Man knew that in a short time he would abandon the flower-radiant hillsides of Galilee, the ministry that had only begun, the people who clamored for hope and healing. Soon he would set his face to the south, toward Jerusalem, the fortress city symbolic of Israel's rise and decline among the nations of the world.

The entire cosmos felt the mounting tempo.

That which had never been was converging on that which had always been. Love and wrath were knit together in one garment; a new light burned and Jesus was transfigured while Peter, James, and John watched in amazement. Upon the mountain the three disciples saw Jesus talking with Moses and Elijah; the Messiah, whom they did not understand, whom they even feared, stood in perfect union with the law and the prophets. The fire of holy history illuminated that mountaintop much as a single star had enlivened the Bethlehem sky. Every prior insight regarding Yahweh's relationship with the creation—deliverance, judgment, law, covenant—poured into that transfiguration. The crescendo was building: Crisis was certain. The three to whom this was revealed were uneasy. And the vision was followed by a voice saying: This is my beloved Son; listen to him.

But Jesus charged them to tell no one what they had seen.

The moment had not yet arrived for sudden and dangerous entry into the jaws of the lion. For a time, therefore, the Son of Man continued to work miracles and to preach Yahweh's kingdom. Also he sent the disciples to preach among the people.

I tell you that Elijah has come, and they did to him whatever they pleased.

The fugitive band traveled across the countryside, moving toward Jerusalem, following and listening to the Word, which was not yet fully spoken. The disciples bore witness to Jesus' centered, lucent Yahweh-faithfulness as they felt themselves plunging forward, careening and lurching through newly created space.

The followers of Jesus were caught in God's whirlwind.

Though they knew the Stranger through his words and actions, none could penetrate the mystery of his person. Chronological details and so-called verifiable facts of history played no part whatsoever in the Jesus encounter—so radical was the course taken, so total was the commitment exacted. Speaking with an authority that both confounded and offended his listeners, Jesus Christ evoked unconditional decision. A person could follow him or reject him, but idle speculation would not suffice. The Christ event questioned every answer, demanded commitment, condemned hypocrisy.

Who is my mother and who are my brothers? Here are my mother and my brothers! For whoever does the will of my Father in heaven is my brother, and sister, and mother.

Yet when the Syro-Phoenician woman sought Jesus in the Gentile regions of Tyre and Sidon, he at first rejected her, refusing to listen, saying he was sent only to the lost sheep of Israel; that was at first. Exhausted by the urgent impossibility of his mission, Jesus lashed out at her, saying that he would not waste the Word, the bread of heaven, on Canaanites. But Yahweh spoke to the Anointed One through the words of this foreigner who stubbornly knelt on the hard ground: "Yes, Lord, yet even the dogs eat the crumbs that fall from their master's table."

The Servant was to suffer for the iniquities of *all*.

Yahweh, Creator and Redeemer, would not tolerate exclusivity or pietism or divisiveness. Thus, Jesus *repented* and with newfound understanding and pity and compassion healed the woman's daughter as she had requested.

Whosoever would be great among you must be your servant, and whosoever would be first among you must be your slave; even as the Son of Man came not to be served, but to serve.

The cosmic turbulence brought about by the entrance of Mystery into the world caused many to fear, expect, even hope for, the end of human existence. The last day seemed imminent. And indeed it was. But what was about to end was not human life.

8

Never again would he see Nazareth.

Nazareth, where he grew to manhood and where later the people sought to kill him. Nazareth, the Galilean town bordered by ancient cave dwellings. No, we are not so far removed from primitive peoples, nor they from our computer technology. At its core, humanity cries out to the Infinite, trembles in the face of massive reality shifts, probes everywhere for meaning and significance. Thus, a child's miraculously preserved skeleton, buried in sediments, is uncovered by seekers after the Mystery. And it was on behalf of this primeval child that Jesus eluded capture and continued preaching and hid himself and waited, waiting until time had nearly ruptured.

We are not so very far removed from the past. Not at all. Those of us who participate in creation live in the company of everyone and everything that has ever been. Our own present voices are mingled with those of ancient tribal hunters who once stalked the dark, uncorrupted wilderness. And on the roads that led through Samaria to Jerusalem, the Man for Others carried with him the lives and the deaths of all the bewildered and suffering former ones and also the lives and the deaths of all those amazed and frightened future ones as yet unborn. The bones and sinews beneath his skin strained and nearly broke with the burden of human transgression. Then, as chronology and eternity approached one another at ever-quickening velocity, Jesus grew half-crazy with bitter urgency and numinous rage.

Foxes have holes, and birds of the air have nests; but the Son of Man has nowhere to lay his head.

By means of shrewdness and military skill, King David had captured Jerusalem from the Canaanites. Now the Incarnate Word selected that same geographical locus as the real place in real time where the Suffering Servant would be numbered with the transgressors and would make of himself an offering for the sins of the whole world. Jesus prepared to lay down his life on behalf of creation. And already orders had gone out for the arrest and capture of the Son of Man.

The Fugitive moved in sober twilight.

Halfway around the world from Judea, there are bones projecting from cliffs and valleys and river beds. The planet alternately buries and uncovers life: many worlds inhabit the same space. What once was has reappeared in another form; death breeds life. The future is created out of the past. And each of us carries the responsibility for cultivation, nurture, of the entire planet—this corner of galactic energy.

In the scorching sunlight of a Middle Eastern desert place did Yahweh walk among us.

God-mystery shrouds these questions: Why then and there? How? Why not another place? Why not another time? Yahweh's Christ event offers no answer. The Word of God poses its own thundering questions: Why anything? Why anyone? Where were you when I laid the foundation of the earth? Tell me, if you have understanding, who determined its measurements—surely you know! Have you commanded the morning since your days began, and caused the dawn to know its place?

Testimony to Jesus is inextricably bound up with historical accounts about the man from Nazareth. But those caught in the whirlwind of the Word-become-flesh were concerned primarily with the story, not with sequence or factual detail. Chronology had splintered, and its myriad shards were sent hurtling through space like reflected light. Jesus brought the fire of Yahweh to people who groped about in shadow—people not so unlike the ancient cave dwellers. To those frustrated or embittered by the opacity that prevents us from discerning historical Jesus, God has spoken: Have the gates of death been revealed to you, or have you seen the

gates of deep darkness? Where is the way to the dwelling of
light, and where is the place of darkness?

The tragedies and joys of every generation were trapped
within a swirling, twisting storm of divine destiny. Pilgrims
who traveled the roads to Jerusalem for Passover were
hardly aware that the sky had already begun to darken, but
in Jericho palm trees shuddered as the Stranger passed by.
Demonic forces moved quickly away from the storm. Feeding on the fears engendered by this dangerous, uncompromising One, they plotted his death.

9

To follow Christ is to lose all sense of proportion.

A wall of violent faith smashed against the world's rationality. Two natures, human and divine, drew near to the
waiting minions of the devil. As he did long ago in the
wilderness, the Remnant One climbed to a height from
which he could see the temple and towers and gates of the
city: Jerusalem, the glory and the downfall of Israel. With
grim fury, Crisis swept down from the Mount of Olives into
a valley where the people had gathered. And the very stones
cried out, crying, Hosanna! as palm branches covered the
road. Yahweh's presence menaced and elated and uprooted
the people: Lo, your king comes to you; triumphant and
victorious is he, humble and riding on an ass, on a colt the
foal of an ass. On this day Zechariah's prophecy was
fulfilled.

But the crowd did not know what they were witnessing.

And the world turned inside out, reversing itself; Yahweh's intrusion (Hosanna!) was shimmering, streaming, stalking. Creation groaned in travail, giving birth to God's high time. Meaninglessness, hopelessness, sin, and atrocity were shredded and shredded (Hosanna in the highest!) by the unflinching, ruthless headwind of God. Garments were strewn along the way before the king who was not a king. Human suffering was about to be sanctified. Evil and death were about to be overthrown. The erupting tempest of God entered Jerusalem as the universe itself shouted, crying: Hosanna, Son of David! Blessed is he who comes in the name of the Lord! Hosanna in the highest!

IV. Not by Searching, Not by Waiting

Behold, I go forward, but he is not there; And backward, but I cannot perceive him; On the left hand I seek him, but I cannot behold him; I turn to the right hand, but I cannot see him. But he knows the way that I take.

—JOB 23:8–10

1

To preach Jesus Christ and him crucified and raised from the dead unto everlasting life by the Lord God of Hosts, raised from the dead, recognizably the crucified one, Jesus: this is the task of those who sense in the Christ event an abrupt intervening, a new awareness of Yahweh's covenant power to transform all things by lifting them up to the glory of God. That the world might know. That finally the dying world that is even yet empty with waiting might know, really know, God with us. Not only in fire and rising smoke or law or in judgment and wrath or in mighty rushing wind, or in the prophets or steadfast love or mercy or still small voice, but *with us* know God, Living God. And not a matter of words either (or ever) such preaching. Not words. A matter of words it is not, but a matter of life and death to preach Jesus Christ and him crucified.

The gospel begins with death.

Jesus rehearsed death again and again throughout his life: he died to childhood in the temple; in the desert he died to ambition; later in Nazareth he died to family; at Gethsemane it was to hope that he died. If we follow Jesus' life only through to its harsh Good Friday conclusion (unbearable outrage), then we see human existence as no more than protracted crucifixion—worthless, random, bitter. And the world has decisively won the day, with death on a cross writing the indictment of all breath, an epitaph of folly and of suffering and of pain. Divine compassion, it would seem, has been waylaid, detoured, diverted in an endless hall of mirrors.

My God, my God, why hast thou forsaken me?

Gospel proclamation begins with death. As always, we try to avert our eyes from the abusiveness of humanity, the senseless tragedy. Coarse, finite, prideful human beings, we wander through unyielding darkness. We build structures of security that Yahweh bombards and bombards until finally they fracture and give way. Our days are like an evening shadow; we wither away like grass. Newspapers scream of death, giving apocalyptic accounts of megaton bombs and nuclear winter. The powerful ones, inattentive and unapproachable, trivialize human struggle: Satan caters to our desires for diversion and serenity. Thus, the spiritual journey must always go where maggots feed and children cry out and hellfire consumes every remaining hope. (But no spiritual journey has ever been made by a spirit.) And crucified truth mourns in that secret, desolate place where Jesus is collapsed and silenced and dead, along with childhood and faith and half a million dreams that might have been.

We do not find God; God finds us.

It has always been so. Therefore, on the third day, the celestial promise, which had not yet been revealed, broke out of the tomb, rattling the incredulous teeth of Satan. Yahweh rolled away the stone and raised Jesus from the dead, showering the universe and beyond with God-purpose and divine fullness and holy glory rainbows of radiant, effulgent dream-colors. Human history ceased, paused, then began again. Uncomprehending, wondering disciples looked upon the countenance of the Holy One, broke bread with Yahweh Sabaoth; creation was healed, freed from bondage, recreated. But resurrection did not bring human perfection or immortality. On the contrary. By raising Jesus from the dead, Yahweh affirmed our imperfection, mortality, vulnerability, tragedy.

Sin and death were not eradicated.

In the Christ event God revealed death as overture, prelude, to glorious symphonic life over life, living dimension that now is and is forever yet to be. Thus are we called to exceed ourselves in faith, to celebrate death and life and resurrection's undefeat, and all the while announcing that death belongs to life and life to God and God to God belongs. Dressed and draped in the colors of mourning, the people of the new creation lay full claim to a strange, disturbing, transformed faith in Yahweh of Covenants, the snarling, attacking, animal-like God: the people proclaim that it is God-in-Christ who conquers all darkness, heals every wound, atones for the sins of the world.

Through resurrection of the Remnant One, we are reaffirmed in spirit/flesh unity with all those who have gone before and with everyone who is yet to be. We are made one in the body of Christ, and the entire body of creation is sanctified, made holy, by the sacrifice of Incarnate God. It is not true that we can participate in mystical union with the

Unsynonymous. But resurrection tore down any and all bar-
riers dividing creation from itself. Out of resurrection consciousness comes the insight that each creature mystically
partakes of Christ's *earthly* nature. And in that earthly nature
the Infinite became finite, took on the stuff of existence, said
Yes to the despairing courage and unfailing God-alignment
of Jesus, the Christ, fully human, suffering.

We are very members incorporate in the mystical body of
Christ.

For no apparent reason, this planet came into being—was
fashioned amid swirling galactic dust and interstellar gases.
Earth's often-violent progress through deep space was carefully watched and monitored and influenced by the Holy
and Terrible One. But why? All this way, all this long way
have we come without ever knowing, without ever once
knowing.

And the resurrection of Jesus Christ is not the logical
conclusion of anything. The Christ event did not result in
the discovery of a great truth. Nor can resurrection be arrived at by means of deductive or inductive reasoning. In a
manner of speaking, the whole thing does not make any *sense*
at all. Our legacy is nothing other than the corporate and
individual experience (and memory) of God's nonrational
intrusion into creation history—primarily in the life, death,
and resurrection of Jesus Christ. And though we must set
forth ideas and beliefs as part of the teaching (theologizing)
task, the ideas do little more than grasp after Yahweh,
snatching at scraps of wind. Neither the intellectual nor the
spiritual quest can succeed in penetrating the mystery of the
Holy One, who is creating still, who is even now redeeming

the heart and the spirit of existence, who knows the creation and passionately loves the creation, who knows and is partly known: the nourishing, uncompromising Other.

We proclaim the Lord of history, who stands responsible for emptiness and fullness, for sin and redemption, for the vast galaxies and the lilies of the field. Our testimony is that in Jesus Christ humankind witnessed the Word crashing through time, exploding the forces of evil: nothing could hold back the snarling outrage of Yahweh Sabaoth.

2

As the veil of the temple was torn asunder, the sky darkened, fragmented, shrieked aloud; Satan's stranglehold on earth broke loose.

Every evil was nailed to that Cross, vanquished by the strength of Unfathomable Wounder and Healer, vanquished by the weakness of irreconcilable Jesus broken, so human and forsaken. For a moment suspended it appeared that Yahweh had disowned the creation—until the howling, fiery, wolf-like One lashed out with full revelation (paradoxical, sunlight-invested, hard-shock Easter morning) and, for the first and only time, human beings looked full upon the face of God.

Father, forgive them; for they know not what they do.

Like Barabbas we have been saved at the last hour. Yet sin has not vanished. We continue to navigate upstream, struggling against the current of our own humanity. Resurrection exposed the finite nature of sin and the unfinished character of death. We can, we must, die to the living world to enter full relationship with the Creator Redeemer God. In Christ the unconditional covenant of Yahweh with all people lived and died and was brought to life again. What happened took creation (even Jesus) by surprise. The Incarnate One held to every faithful human expectation. He preached the immediacy of Almighty God's kingdom, but more than that, he preached Yahweh: the mortal Jesus did not know what was going to happen. And at resurrection all creation gasped at the God-Incarnate revelation that had been true (but unrevealed) since Bethlehem. Neither the particles of matter on Earth nor the clouds of dust floating in space had foreseen the unique, unrepeatable, singular event called resurrection.

What had been approaching space-time since before the first dawn now resonated with the Word of universal grace.

Creation was baptized and the River flowed on; what happened was not the end of the world. Those who expected everything to end were wrong. And the story is not Jesus' story; it is the proclamation of God Incarnate, the announcement of the Creator's seizing and shaking the creation, shaking it to death and to life beyond death—extraordinary, incomprehensible God-love. And the River flows on through desolate and rocky fields, in all directions flowing, reversing the order of time, glinting with moonlight, the inexorable waters of life, tumbling wild across parched dead earth. God is God. And it is a mysterious, shattering, freeing thing to fall into the hands of Yahweh Sabaoth. There is nothing static about the One who rides through the desert. Before the resurrection of Jesus and ever since, men and women of faith have come up against Ultimate Mystery and called that experience God; they have been pursued and turned inside out and therein have recognized Yahweh of

Hosts. The Holy One manifests complex, differentiated, dynamic unity: the God who was revealed to Israel is the triune God of Christian creed and confession.

Any statement about Jesus, therefore, must arise out of Yahweh-consciousness. No disparity exists between the Giver of the Covenants and God Incarnate. Thus, the centrality of Christ occurs at the heart of the One Mystery. We may be apprehended by the Christ or turned around by the Jesus event or broken apart by Crisis. But our faith confesses one God, one covenant, one redemption. Spirit-journey follows a path that parallels the road to Golgotha, an impossible way made possible by the sacrifice of God.

The greatness (and strangeness) of historical Jesus resides in the single, intense focus of his devotion to the One Presence. In Christ was witnessed adoration, gratitude, and passionate commitment to Yahweh; for humanity there was pity. But the Man of Sorrows did not accept people for who they were; he shouted, *Repent!* It is God-in-Christ who redeems and accepts creation—not the human Jesus. What filled the heart and soul and mind of the man from Nazareth was not love but God: not hope, faith, humility, or obedience either. Jesus was only hopeful of God, faithful to Yahweh, humble before the Lord, obedient to the Transcendent One.

Hear, O Israel: The Lord our God, the Lord is one; And you shall love the Lord your God with all your heart, and with all your soul, and with all your mind, and with all your strength.

We celebrate, rehearse, remember, the death of Christ because on Golgotha it was death that died, because the story does not end at the Place of the Skull, because God reached into the tomb and raised Jesus from the dead. And historically, humanity was shaken alive, reborn; creation was jolted awake, seized by the power of Infinite love.

No longer condemned to solitude and emptiness, we have been driven, prodded, into freedom. To Golgotha Jesus carried the sins of the world, that we might never again be shackled to the past, that we might be free to live, free from the burden of our own sinfulness, free for radical neighbor-love. All of this happened that the world might know, really know, God with us.

Yet we cry out that human life is of few days and full of trouble. Surrounded by possessions, entertained and manipulated by electronic signals, this generation seeks not a sign but information. We violate privacy. We create instant fame and celebrity. And each day the manipulators insinuate, persuade, their way into our decision making. They encourage global numbness, detachment from the world's pain, withdrawal into limbo-self. Like sheep we huddle in dread, anticipating an Armageddon for which we will not take responsibility. A shadow has been cast on the planet, we cry. Oh, a shadow has been cast on planet Earth, all right, but it is not the shadow of the Evil One. Moreover, if Armageddon comes, it will be a holocaust of our own making.

Why do you not understand what I say? It is because you cannot bear to hear my word. You are of your father the devil, and your will is to do your father's desires. He was a murderer from the beginning, and has nothing to do with the truth, because there is no truth in him.

A shadow has been cast. It is the figure of Yahweh, whose Christ event even now is judging the iniquities of the people. Know this: God will not back down. The evil of our generation does not frighten the Maker of heaven and earth. Nor will God be mocked. Every pretense of noninvolvement will clatter to the ground, and humanity shall stand frail and stunned and redeemed before Yahweh Sabaoth, the Holy One who has not led us into the wilderness that we might starve. We will be spiritually fed as the five thousand were fed, delivered from bondage and delivered again. The absolutely inescapable price of our freedom has been paid in full; but now the cost is the cost of discipleship. By resurrection Yahweh proclaims that salvation is not dependent upon good works or upon depth of understanding. Grace is bestowed regardless of merit or knowledge. Nevertheless, we find ourselves pushed and pushed by the Triune One to repentance, to faith, to God-alignment.

I am the bread of life; those who come to me shall not hunger and those who believe in me shall not thirst.

As Moses fed the people with manna, which they did not know, so did the Christ bring a new form of nourishment, that in this present we might experience God's high time, feed upon the spiritual food of redemption-promise, and be reborn of the Spirit.

Humanity holds some sort of peculiar fascination, significance, for the Lord of time. We are incredibly important to the working-out of divine destiny.

Much as Earth orbits the sun, so the sun carries all of its planets, moons, and asteroids on a vast journey around the entire galaxy. This immense caravan moves up, then down (relative to a hypothetical galactic plane), making a complete circuit every 250 million years. We are not alone. We travel in the company of primordial stars, bright explosive comets, ubiquitous floating matter. And every last created particle has been and yet shall be redeemed, healed, affirmed, by Yahweh of Hosts. In truth, while we rehearse our creeds, the solar system edges its way outward, exactly outward bound. Whenever we partake of the holy mysteries, we carry with us, there and then, the deaths of multitudinous silent implacable stars, the brokenness of all life in every time, every galaxy. The people of the new creation are indeed strange creatures who know themselves to be received by Almighty God, valued by the Eternal Unsynonymous Other.

Consider the lilies of the field, how they grow; they neither toil nor spin; yet I tell you, even Solomon in all his glory was not arrayed like one of these.

Those who follow Yahweh (the Fiddler on the Roof) will always be off-balance, precariously situated between this world and the next. We are creatures of analogy and paradox and madness.

3

Perhaps it was because we did not believe, or because we could not.

When they had finished breakfast, the woman and the man and the little boy left the diner. The man carried their suitcases through gray, stubborn rain across flooded streets, leaning hard against the forces of hard luck and steady disaster. "How far is it?" she shouted at the inflexible figure ahead. She said it without expectation of answer, perhaps believing that the sound of her voice would confer reality upon the nondescript, too-long 4:00 A.M. streets. Whenever the child stopped walking, she picked him up. It was as if she had spent every day of the last eight years trudging those rainy streets, carrying the boy and following the man. At the bus station they stood near the ticket counter, faces wet, immobile. "Do we have enough?" the woman said, saying it not to the young man behind the wire-mesh screen but to the pile of crumpled bills and greasy coins on the counter. "Three to St. Louis?" the ticket seller asked. A second time she said, "Do we have enough?" Dirty water fell from her dress to the linoleum floor. Her eyes looked as hard and worn as the coins she stared at. Behind the screen, the ticket seller shifted uneasy on his leather stool. The large black-and-white clock on the station wall jerked one more minute past four o'clock. Then for the third time she said, "Do we have enough?" and the ticket seller scooped the money out of sight. Then he pushed something toward them. "Three tickets to St. Louis," he said. "Gate five."

Grace sustains everything that is. And grace may strike in the dark hours—but the night will not give up its darkness. Because grace isn't a magic power. Nor does it bestow forgiveness or reward. What does take place is a slight shifting of the folds within space-time that allows for momentary perception of Yahweh's awesome, holy loving-kindness.

The ancient witness does not disclose a plan for anyone's life. It testifies to a living relationship, a peculiar bond, between the fragile, trembling creation and Ultimate Purpose. Our forebears identified certain historical events as the mighty acts of God. By faith they differentiated, distinguished among divine attributes or powers such as Spirit, Wisdom, and Word. The ancient witness is this: There are not three Gods or many Gods. Yahweh our God is one

Yahweh; every experience of the Holy One is an experience of the totality of divine power. We use the trinitarian formula as a means of speaking about various ways in which God is God—to distinguish and to correlate what is revealed in divine activity. We are neither demarcating three different kinds of experiences nor attempting to reconcile the divinity of Christ with Israel's monotheism. Each person of the Trinity refers to the whole of the Godhead; each is Totally Other and each is Incarnate God.

The living reality of Yahweh cannot be shaped or structured by philosophical overlay.

Resurrection gospel (good news) demands that we announce, define, teach, explicate what never in this life can be made clear or explicit. Even at Easter the opacity between *here* and *there* did not burn off like mist in the morning sun. Those who told of it, who tried to articulate historical resurrection and the subsequent experience of resurrection-community, spoke in terms of Son and Spirit and Father. But the unity of Yahweh was both affirmed and assumed. Christian testimony gives eloquent witness to the rich, dynamic character of radical monotheism.

Thus has the great tradition been transmitted. And we hear the voice of the Lord saying: Whom shall I send and who will go for us? We are the people of the story—the few who proclaim on behalf of the many that where alienation once ruled, there is now healing; where we once believed ourselves estranged from God, there is now living covenant. Of necessity, we are interpreters of the faith.

We become theologians.

The resurrection of Jesus took place in chronology, but it shattered time-sequence. It belongs within the order of events called holy history; it is also utterly unique, singular, never-before-or-since, and arbitrary. The final triumph of God began with resurrection. Ultimate redemption of the created order commenced, and sacramental meaning intruded upon every material reality. By its very comprehensiveness, the revelation of God in Resurrected Christ restated the impenetrability of Holy Mystery.

Unequivocally, we affirm historical resurrection.

But what startled, offended the world was not historicity. What startled were the myriad implications of the event called resurrection, i.e., Yahweh's *direct* self-disclosure and the impossibility of incarnation. Every time-bound event is unique and unrepeatable. However, the theological statement that issued forth from this particular event enabled creation of a new community that celebrated death as the portal to life. Know this: The disciples did not reassemble after crucifixion, bound together by a sudden *esprit de corps.* The followers of Jesus were dragged out of holes they had dug for themselves in the aftermath of Good Friday; it was the Resurrected Christ who re-called them, re-membered the body. Those who witnessed what took place in succeeding years—Greek and Roman and Jew alike—were astonished and dismayed. Faith that could endure that kind of persecution must certainly be based on tangible, experienced, historical reality. Moreover, the community declared that the sacrifice of One held significance far beyond the body gathered, the *ecclesia*—significance that extended even unto the borders of creation.

4

The smell of eternity lingered in the air at Jerusalem, on the road to Emmaus, on the shores of the Lake of Galilee. The community gathered and wondered and set about with pneumatic zeal to preach the Word of grace. The moiling chaos of Holy Week had ended in death. But now, joy (not happiness)—severe, life-enabling joy based on sure and certain hope—had overcome grief and heartbroken despair.

In the desert a camel caravan lurches its way toward an ancient crossroads where visitors intrude upon the thin existence of that place. Children beg. Food in the open market is covered with black flies. Dust on ageless streets covers the blood from centuries of proud warfare. But those who were once fierce nomads now sit near carved wooden doors that still bear the marks of spears wielded by their ancient grandfathers. At night uncanny music surrounds the starvation of many and the opulence of few. Earthly passage through history remembers, then forgets, the outposts, the wretched oases of another time. Visitors who curse the inexorable sun or the sudden violent sandstorms have forfeited the exhilarating mystery of a reality that clings to existence for as long as there is water to drink or food to eat.

To embrace such reality is to be overtaken by the freedom of Yahweh.

So it was that when the day of Pentecost had come, they were all together in one place. And a sound came from heaven like the rush of a mighty wind, and it filled all the house where they were sitting. And there appeared to them tongues as of fire, distributed and resting on each one of them.

The apprehended presence of God, the experience of Tri-une Unity, comes in glory and in terror, by means of the ongoing beat of life and the shattering of illusions. The early community was filled with vibrant awareness of Yahweh's covenant-love; it was plunging headlong into a world lethal with anger and offense and unbelief. Forces that could not bear the power of Jesus Christ and him crucified, forces that hated the community of the resurrection, were readying more crosses, preparing to crush that community's triumphant witness.

Jesus was sentenced to death for claiming (in words and symbolic actions) to be God's messiah, the expected earthly agent of Yahweh Sabaoth. This claim he made. Though Jesus did not profess to be Incarnate God, he spoke openly on behalf of Yahweh, lived out the Suffering Servant prophecy, and finally committed his death by riding a donkey into Jerusalem at the time of Passover in deliberate fulfillment of Zechariah 9:9. In the life of Jesus, Yahweh (who cannot participate in sin) was immersed in original sin. The two natures of Christ brought about the incarnation of Glory and the sanctification of separation. Moreover, the Man for Others was many times tempted unto personal sin. But ultimately, at resurrection, the fire of sinlessness burned away even that temptation to estrangement. Thus did the sinless Incarnate Christ know sin. And while yet human, fully human drawn, did the Wholly Other remain without spot of sin fully God, Holy Living Presence, One.

We know that creation groaned in travail, waiting for the eschaton (end times), searching the skies for a sign, waiting. Then salvation entered like a thief in the night, robbing Satan of his power. The clashing with tragedy and chaos was unavoidable.

But we are not victims of a malicious God. Neither are we visitors who bear no responsibility, carry no burden. Entrusted by Yahweh with planet Earth—a pearl of great price —human beings are colleagues and co-creators with God, albeit broken and sinful ones. Clearly the human predicament is neither simple nor one-dimensional. We are called upon to make impossible decisions, endure relentless suffering, navigate perilous waters where the currents change quickly. Rather than clutching at simple explanations of what is in truth unfathomable, we do better to grapple directly with the darkness, looking always toward the Transcendent One. Passionate God-service involves participation in swift-rushing high time—experiencing the everywhere uncertainty and gnawing fear of blindness with full-open eyes and mind, always asking why.

A bell rings from an unknown direction, the sound phantomlike in mist.

It is Yahweh alone who sanctifies; sanctification (making holy of all creation) belongs to God, who from the beginning chose us for salvation. Sanctification is already ours. It ought not to be understood as an activity but rather as a given, a presupposition of the Creator's passion for the finite order, a passion revealed most fully in the Christ event. God-awareness begins with sanctification. But it is also manifest in loving response to the redemptive intrusion of Infinite Other. Sanctification is both complete and incomplete. Yahweh calls for obedience; but the Lord God is in no way dependent upon our ability to respond.

The sacrifice of Christ disclosed the awful truth that Yahweh heals while we are yet destroying, redeems those who revile God, sanctifies our irreverence.

5

In Christ, the Holy One tasted death, then consumed, devoured the power of it, breaking apart, shattering, scattering creature-despair at last. The common fate of humanity was exchanged for resurrection.

As in Adam all die, so in Christ shall all be made alive.

Within the world of existence, death symbolizes separation from God; it represents incontrovertible falling away from Life. But we have been baptized into the death of Christ; we have crossed the Red Sea and are now in mid-desert; to us the triumphant Word has been announced. He is risen! The Lord is risen indeed!

An entire life based on maddeningly little knowledge and even less faith. And here she was, staring around the corner at fifty. Just a moment earlier she had been thinking beyond the shadowed windows, thinking: *I hope there is nothing I have to decide. That's what. I hope there is nothing.* Then they came out. But she was not listening to them because she knew it already. The whole passel of them came out into the waiting room. But she was not watching. She was still thinking: *I hope*

I don't have to decide, while word by word the questions struck
at her. A maelstrom of faces told her. Then the water glass
she was holding fell to the floor, shivering into a thousand
antiseptic fragments. And the accident, the child, the sur-
gery. What about it? For forty-nine and a half years she had
kept her passions and sorrows safely contained. Now she
was tired and could not listen to that which she already
knew, with the night disappearing and the heartbeat within
her knowing that the child had been deprived of oxygen for
too many minutes. Without once listening she knew. Something sudden had interposed between her and the child.
Something of her own breath there was also that followed
along in measured cadence breathing, thinking: *Why should I
understand now? I have never understood. Good Lord, no, I have never
until this moment understood. I didn't even know it when he was growing
up. So why should I understand now?* And the waiting ones stared
at her pain; the invincible physicians washed their hands of
the decision. She was there with all around her too the
shattered glass. "Why?" she said. And none to answer either
in that antiseptic, shadowed place. It was not they she asked,
besides, who blended away to the oxygenless, flat, black
thought: *Because he isn't dead. But I can kill him.* (It was not they
she asked.) Then after a time, the thought and the room and
the faces vanished. And she, looking at nothing, speaking
with a flat, distant voice, said: "He is my son, you know."
It was November when she said the words. Outside fell slow
steady gray rain.

6

The Word of God must never be understood to be the
words of human witness. We who tell the story are en-
meshed in sin; our souls are sick to death with condemnation

and blame and hardness of heart. The wind and the waves of opposition have dragged us down into doubt-oblivion. It is Yahweh alone who can break through the worldly ramparts we build, who can destroy the power of the demonic. By grace are we freed to tell the story in spite of our own unworthiness. Because of God's self-disclosure, especially in the life, death, and resurrection of Jesus Christ, we shout (audaciously, passionately) that the universe has been healed; every man, woman, and child on the face of the Earth is free to let go of the past. And whereas we have carried on our backs the burden of past transgressions and have sentenced ourselves to spiritual death, the Triune God has declared it is high time for us to get on with our lives. We are free to live. There is no exception: each life is utterly significant in that it has been given value by Almighty God.

We are called upon to *live our lives* with whatever gifts have been granted. Children are not exempted on the grounds that they are too young. A retarded child bestows on the world an unceasing sense of wonder in the face of adult cynicism. A sixth-grader finds his mother, who has been abandoned in a hospital corridor, and refuses to leave until the doctors take responsibility. It is enough. Yahweh summons all creatures to abundant life. Sooner or later, each of us will get out of the boat and walk through the waves as Peter did.

God-encounter snatches away security, shoves human beings up against the stark realities of finitude and unmitigated limitation. There is no escape. If we run away as Jonah did, Yahweh will hunt us down until we can run no longer. But if we die to the world, cast our idols to the ground, and turn to the Giver of life, we shall find ourselves suddenly, unaccountably free. Those who know freedom in the Lord are the ones who have experienced the awesome, crushing, liberating hand of God and, in the wake of that experience, have said *Yes* to reality. These are the ones who recognize that every human gesture has eternal significance. Caught in the cruciformity of time, they are real people, living real lives, buffeted by the headwind of God.

The freedom of the Holy One smashes, destroys demon-power.

Many of us choose to ignore the warning signs of divine judgment, especially as interpreted by the prophets; others seek to kill whatever threatens their idols. But the lucid ones (Spirit people) immerse themselves in history, affirming the triumph of grace over sin. And they are myriad: this great cloud of witnesses includes women and men and children from every age. They are the broken ones who have come to know that the only gift they have to give is the gift of their death, who have embraced holy insecurity, trusting to that which cannot be proven, hoping in that which cannot be seen. In each of them breathes the totality of creation; each life extends into every past and every future. And the decision to say *Yes* to imperfect, ever-shifting creation does not go unheeded. The Word ripples away on behalf of the one in a thousand thousand, extending outward, turning, overturning tables of corruption, standing present to the struggle of one frightened child. The people of the story encounter the complex, dynamic, differentiated Yahweh and choose life in the midst of death. It is in dying to illusion that their lives are given back to them; through repentance comes freedom.

But the demonic does not disappear—illusion is part of the fabric of the world.

Today our corporate life is being destroyed by the illusion that street people are degenerate, shiftless, subhuman. A transient is assaulted, cornered against a fence by the driver of a pickup truck. Vagrants who sleep under bridges and who inhabit city parks become targets for the hostility and violence of otherwise peaceful citizens. Why? Perhaps we cannot stand to see the blood-naked need that is embodied in these wretched homeless men and women. Our most common responses are to ignore or to attack. But those who have embraced the reality of Yahweh's creation have been freed to celebrate vulnerability, to bring about societal change. Bearing witness to the incarnation, Spirit people announce that, by analogy, we encounter God in the woman who sleeps each city winter night on a sidewalk steam vent. Yahweh's presence hovers in the essential and ineradicable homelessness of humankind. And the judgment of God falls upon anyone who would further divide the world from itself by renouncing the poor and the dispossessed.

The Christ event exposes us in all of our limitation. Yet by repentance (turning toward the Source of All) we perceive shattering Christ-encounter as freedom. Thoroughgoing neighbor love, unsentimental caring for one another, follows.

When the world's financial system wavers on the edge of destruction, it is the Spirit of the Lord that grinds us down, revealing the illusion of unbridled spending, fracturing the idol of profiteering, freeing the nations to acknowledge interdependence. The squeeze of historical God-encounter affords humankind the opportunity for repentance. And resurrection demonstrates that Yahweh's power far exceeds that of death or evil or suffering. The Triune God does not seek to punish or destroy; grace abounds.

Wherever finitude is overcome by the Infinite, there is occasion for rejoicing.

A nurse whose paralyzed three-year-old daughter cannot return her embrace lives each day with the ongoing mystery of that child, and grace sustains an impossible battle to bring movement to unmoving limbs. The task is humanly impossible: ordinary dreams have vanished; in their place resides unimaginable, severe joy in the unique life of a three-year-old girl.

When physicians rise up and assume a prophetic role in order to denounce the lie of survivable nuclear war, the rushing wind of Yahweh goes before. On that wind are pleas from schoolchildren and entertainers and bishops; people who have shaken loose from the demon of isolationism are refusing to accept the necessity of world destruction; the voices on the wind are growing in number, demanding cooperation among nations, denouncing covert war efforts. The prophet of God has become a corporate body. Eternal Unsynonymous Power is gathering up people of faith and people of unfaith. As the myths of society (progress, upward mobility, exploitation of irreplaceable resources) crumble, individual human beings are impelled to forge new images. The Holy One is calling us to the task of recreating civilization. Each of us has been confronted by the Word: Arise, take up your bed and walk! God-in-Christ and Christ in the

Spirit (all holy, transcendent, divergent Oneness) has decreed the creation to be already sanctified; Yahweh has not disinherited or discarded us. We shall repent. And the storm that we fought and could not conquer will become the wind that sustains and empowers us. The invisible, destructive, life-giving breath of God moves through the world at will. First the zephyr, then the whirlwind enters historical order: the Spirit is dynamic, creative, life-and-death-experienced.

7

Rudimentary shelters of woven grass border the town where food is to be distributed. Women and men wait with empty sacks. Hopeless-eyed, emaciated children watch the horizon. And a news photographer makes a solitary, decisional response: he captures the somber, dying faces on film, then fights for publication of that awful testimony. But when finally the world learns of, wakes up to, that ongoing famine-death, years have passed and thousands have starved: those who survive have been sustained by the spirit-freedom of the myriad souls, living and dead, who ruthlessly shook humankind out of its apathy. These intentional ones acted, consciously or unconsciously, as imperfect, historical instruments of Yahweh Sabaoth. And the task of feeding all the inhabitants of planet Earth will be accomplished by individuals who refuse to absolve any nation or group of responsibility—while struggling daily with their own sinfulness and that of the entire world. Those who feed the Earth will be the nameless, faceless ones who continue to walk through the wind and across the waves. Spirit people know they are dying their deaths on behalf of creation so the world might live: to keep rendezvous with the Lord of history requires dying daily to illusion, standing present to the impossibility of the task, remaining faithful to the One who disperses and gathers up.

We do not live to ourselves or die to ourselves. If we live, we live to the Lord, and if we die, we die to the Lord.

The people of the new creation declare that no sacrifice, no life, has ever been offered in vain. Nor can Satan reverse the thunderous, rushing advance of God's redemption. God-in-Christ will not allow humankind to give itself over to the powers of evil. Tired and frightened as we may be, we are called to do the impossible. We are called to create a future for our children. It is on behalf of Yahweh that we reject the lie that says nuclear war is inevitable. In the name of God we repent of isolationism and insularity, knowing that the future of the entire creation rests on the shoulders of each individual. And from the Wholly Other we receive the enabling, uncomfortable, glorious Word. Nothing in heaven or on earth can separate us from the steadfast love of God, who has declared all life to be valuable and received.

By raising Jesus from the dead, Yahweh revealed the good news of accomplished redemption begun.

The stone which the builders rejected has become the head of the corner; the Christ event holds together all of holy history, from Genesis to the final days. But the glorious revelation of God-in-Christ is also the rock that falls upon and grinds into dust the principalities and powers of this world. Incarnate God was shattered and shattered and then reformed as the revealed foundation of new being. Peter is not the rock upon which the new community was founded;

the one foundation is Yahweh-Spirit-Christ. A voice cries: Our forebears were all under the cloud, and all passed through the sea, and all were baptized into Moses in the cloud and in the sea, and all ate the same supernatural food and all drank the same supernatural drink. For they drank from the supernatural Rock which followed them, and the Rock was Christ. There was never a time that did not know Christ. Yahweh is alpha and omega, cornerstone and capstone, foundation and fulfillment. Every idolatry flees in terror from the Word; but in repentance all children discover a shelter from the wind, the shade of a great rock in the weary land. The Lord growls over the world, undaunted by the screams of Satan. Like birds hovering, Yahweh of Hosts protects creation. And the words of the prophet: Turn to the Holy One from whom you have deeply revolted, O people of the covenant.

We are not dead, we are only sleeping; nothing in this world can prevent the Triune God from taking us by the hand and awakening the spirit within us.

The testimony is this: Therefore since we are surrounded by so great a cloud of witnesses, let us lay aside every weight, and sin which clings so closely, and let us run with perseverance the race that is set before us.

At a moment when our nation's survival absolutely depends on the survival of other nations, world leaders are being assassinated. Hostage taking has become routine. Schools and churches and mosques are mown down by the machinery of guerrilla warfare. A passenger train is blown up just before Christmas Day; terrorist organizations stumble over each other in claiming responsibility for the explosion. Violence is the predominant drug of the waning century. If an adult foster-care unit moves into a neighborhood, the facility is apt to be bombed or set on fire. Struggling against the world's sinfulness, Spirit people find themselves surrounded by real danger: quite literally, they risk death in the work of the Lord.

8

Rend your hearts and not your garments, says the Lord. Return to me with all your heart.

Faith necessarily involves repentance, turning away from sin, reorientation of heart and soul and mind toward the One God. A voice cries: Among the nations we will find no ease, and there shall be no rest—only a trembling heart and failing eyes and a languishing soul. But the Lord God is an everlasting rock in whom we may trust forever. And, as people of the covenant, our trust is in God alone. Faith is the response of the whole person transformed, listening, repenting.

The Lord has spoken: A new heart I will give you, and a new spirit I will put within you; and I will take out of your flesh the heart of stone and give you a heart of flesh.

Awakened to God's action in history, we become new creatures, no longer searching for God but bringing the Word of hope to all we meet. Moreover, the chronological order is moving through history to a future where God shall ingress again. Ours is a sure and certain hope of salvation by grace through the faithfulness of Christ.

It is only the hope of God's redemption that enables us to stand present, to witness, as a small girl whispers, "I don't want to be an orphan," when, upon coming home, she discovers the blood-soaked bodies of her mother and father and brother and then must live with the dead faces and the sight of her infant brother's body held tight in the arms of the mother, who tried to shield him. The mother could not save him from death, and she could not spare her daughter this gruesome, incomprehensible discovery. Only the Maker of heaven and earth can account that infant's sacrifice as part of the necessary story of creation. No human voice can justify the world's evil. But to announce gospel is to assert boldly that everything and everyone partakes of God's saving purpose. Not fate but destiny (with all its implications of destination) determines our lives. We are creatures of meaning; the world is not a planet lost and cut adrift in hostile space. Ultimate Mystery validates the life of a single orphaned child after the same fashion that it sustains the existence of the myriad star clusters comprising the Milky Way.

As we reach out to darkness beyond darkness for an answer that can explain the outpouring of hydrogen atoms from the center of our galaxy, we run up against the Unsynonymous One. The sober desperation of a young boy who commits suicide so there will be one less mouth for his family to feed calls into question every human answer and dispels the sleep of complacence.

We rejoice amid horror. If we cannot find ourselves at Golgotha, then we have yet to be born into this world.

A policewoman fails to return home from the grocery store. Her automobile is found abandoned. Eight months later her husband and children still live suspended somewhere between grief and hope. The rolls of the missing include neighbors and runaways and soldiers and hostages. Words are played and replayed endlessly in the minds of family and friends; blurred photographs are treasured; memories fade silently into more and more distant past. The spirit-journey leaves many people sidelined. Everyone must live some*where,* inside a body-mind complex that is never prepared for what comes. *In this world, things are not right.* We run along the precipice of crisis, balanced on the edge of abyss.

Next year each of our personal universes will be different from what it is now. Deep within there is a vertical time line linking all of the events in our lives—Christmases and birthdays and anniversaries, good and bad memories. Nameless dread permeates present events as they are overlaid on the past. Someone will not be home for Christmas next year; someone will die; something will be missing or added, changing life utterly. Overlaid with the present, the past sighs in wordless grief. The burden of history becomes intolerable. We hear the Christmas hymns and suddenly burst into tears. Brokenness and sin and disease overwhelm the human spirit. We proclaim the birth of the Christ child at Christmas, but it is the weight of the Cross that we experience.

An aroma of bitter spices filled the air in that rude birthing-place; Jesus took on the world's suffering from the moment he was born, as helpless and unprotected from evil as anyone. The human child grown would be nailed and nailed to a cross and then, screaming for God to help him, would despair and believe and die. He did not retreat from the world; he actively committed his death on behalf of all creation. But there was nothing to shield him from pain, nothing. The miracle was his unidirectional, God-centered faith in the horrible midst of suffering.

It is God's raising Jesus from the dead that the church proclaims.

The story brings hope to the hopeless and light into a world where there is great darkness. The story tells of how Yahweh entered space-time, redeeming absurdity and helplessness and atrocity. By resurrection faith we announce that whereas things are not right with the world, God has become at-one with us; atonement has been made. We remember and rehearse the story of that triumph over death; sinful and broken, we allow ourselves to be sustained by the fierce Word of God; we live in faithful expectation of the final freeing (redemption) of the world. This is Yahweh's high time. There is no earthly cure for our human condition. Children will still be missing next year; people will be homeless, incarcerated, diseased. No preparation of body-spirit (soul) can reverse the aging process or prevent a tractor-trailer from jackknifing on icy roads, then colliding with eternity. Everyone is too young to die. And no one ever dies for nothing. Resurrection lifts up, sanctifies the spirit-journey.

Yahweh stepped into a historical tomb and raised Jesus from the dead. The implications of that once-for-all action reached every past and every future.

We need not be forever sidelined, destroyed by the world's power. Everyone travels a spiritual, historical passage from *here* to *there.* Mysteriously, some discover that in accepting reality they are freed to live by faith. Spirit people are of various ages, many creeds, all human families. Directly or indirectly, they proclaim the enabling Word of grace. One cancer victim, a child, expended the last few days of his life bringing strength to fellow patients. From the depths of child-vulnerability came the words: "Go ahead and be scared. Keep a positive attitude always. And most of all—hang tough."

We are free to live—with whatever time has been granted, with whatever gifts have come to us.

Two men had lived on the streets for more than twenty years, protecting each other from the twin terrors of poverty and violence, together finding scraps of food and meager shelter. Then, at last, in the dim light of a frozen dawn, one of them could not be roused. We believe Yahweh will use the sacrifice of that life to the final working-out of divine purpose. Divine purpose working, out on the streets. Covenant-love does not depend on anything human. God does not withhold grace from the hydrocephalic child. There is nothing we can do to secure justification before the Lord of all. We fade like a leaf, and our iniquities, like the wind, scatter us across the earth: all our righteous deeds are like a polluted garment. Then, while we were yet helpless, at the right time, Christ died for the ungodly, for each one of us.

9

Yahweh of Hosts has done what no one could do: not Moses or the prophets or even the human Jesus. God announced that the whole of creation has been healed, brought into right relationship with the Creator. By works of the law shall no one be justified. By grace all may participate in the saving action of the Holy One. We proclaim that we are dead to sin (here and now dying), free to get on with the spirit-journey in sure and certain hope of salvation by grace through Christ's faithfulness as attested to by his resurrection and appropriated by our faith. The story radiates with hope.

People who live in Spirit freedom are always off balance.

We are called upon to give thanks in everything that is. Our journey is like everyone's journey except for the *Yes*. Discipleship demands that we make Eucharist (give thanks, celebrate Christ) even though innocent people are herded into gas chambers. Summit meetings between world powers, scientific breakthroughs, social reform—none has meaning outside the creative activity of God.

It is good to be afraid. Every creature is afraid.

Just as day is breaking, he sits up in bed. "Can't lie here all day," he says. "Got work to do." A wrinkled, palsied hand touches the coverlet. "Where are my clothes, Sarah?" The form in the next bed is silent as smoke. Then a sad blankness comes over him. He says: "Sarah, where is the farm? I don't remember . . ." The roommate, who is not the long-dead Sarah, does not answer, will wait to get up until after the man has left and begun his daily wandering. Time has gradually dissolved. Once or twice a day now he will remember the auction in which the flat red earth he cleared and planted and nursed was sold to a stranger with stained teeth. Only once or twice a day does he remember. Then the memories slide back down into the shifting, foundationless void. It is as if the hourglass of his life had been broken one day, spilling out all the grains of work and love onto the ground. After the sale Sarah had died. That was how he told it until in the telling he became a little dreamy, bemused, his face lowered a little, in the afternoon sitting and talking and then not knowing what it was he was talking about: afternoon and afternoon. Now he asks the same questions hundreds of times over, questions she does not answer, not even in his mind. The space he occupies is familiar with ten years. After lunch he sits near the roommate at one of the long tables that has been cleared of food and plates and flatware. The cabbage smell reminds him of something, though he cannot remember just what instant in seventy-two years has almost edged back into consciousness. He sits quite still, facing the table. "Want to play cards?" he says. The roommate does not talk and every day wears two shirts. It is because he feels time scattering and drifting that the man, who believes more than he knows and knows more than he seems to, sits at the long table, watching the roommate, unmoving. *When will there be nothing left of me?* he says inside, not out loud, because it would frighten to say the words out loud. Instead he says, "Want to play cards?" The roommate turns away, and he still sitting there with time scattering and drifting, drifting and scattering, until at last he gets up with absolute and quiet bemusement, thinking maybe to find another to ask. Then there is a small girl, who apparently has hunted him out from among the others, saying: "Are you my grandpa?" He says, "I don't know." He says it carefully. It seems important to him now not to shout. "I don't think so," he says, and he looks at the small child-face without knowing, and she all the while watching from behind an expression of intense amazement. "Who are you?" she says. "Who am I? Who am I?" he says. And the question hangs suspended in the trembling air as he searches his mind for what he had known so well this morning, while brief tears form, then cease. "I'm a farmer," he says at last. A smile moves on his face when he hears the words. Shuffling her feet back and forth, she says, "Where's your farm?" And he is filled with a sudden fury and despair that he cannot penetrate, that is already falling out of pattern, out of focus, as the auctioneer's gavel comes down again and again on the hourglass. "It's breaking," he says; his head feels intolerably heavy. And he realizes then, still standing there, still watching the child, he senses then that it will happen soon, sooner than he thought, and all around him her voice like in a dream. "I made cupcakes, Grandpa," she says. "I made cupcakes."

At our depths there is only one question that plagues and torments the soul: the question of emptiness and meaninglessness. Will the final word be death and suffering and sin? We have sunk in deep mire where there is no foothold, and the waters have come up to our necks. Will the sacrifice of even a single life be lost in the abyss? Nothing ever changes and nothing remains the same either. And we are those to whom the Word of God came that we might believe in God by the mercy of God.

Take this, God says, and then gives us faith in God.

We, to whom the Word of the Lord came, saying, Arise, prophet! and we thinking, *All this way, all this long way have we come,* and the tears streaming down; thinking, *That's enough now, maybe this will be enough;* thinking, *All this long way and at last the preparation is finished.* But the preparation is not

finished. And God says, Before you were born I consecrated you; I appointed you a prophet to the nations: Arise,
prophet! And we say, We believe in God, thinking, *If only
we knew how to pray, we would pray now.* And the preparation is
not finished yet.

V. On the Run

Therefore, since we are surrounded by so great a cloud of witnesses, let us also lay aside every weight, and sin which clings so closely, and let us run with perseverence the race that is set before us, looking to Jesus the pioneer and perfecter of our faith, who for the joy that was set before him endured the cross, despising the shame, and is seated at the right hand of the throne of God.

—HEBREWS 12:1–2

1

Nothing solely of transient earth can address human need.

We give our children names and little else. Each person must discern between courage and foolhardiness, caution and paranoia. A welfare mother believes that her life is not her own; it belongs to social workers who administrate, to agencies that establish labyrinthine eligibility rules. After a long illness, a teacher watches his life slip down the drain of unemployment. Living human beings are discarded with the day's trash. And almost everyone wants to *act,* to step out of the victim role, to touch the Infinite.

Our mistake is in repressing the outcry, the shriek.

We rail against injustice, evil, fate. But in truth, a fist raised in anger is always a fist raised against God. Yahweh takes responsibility for everything that is—everything. For the most part prayer arises out of selfish concern. It begins with a desire to manipulate God. We want creation to change, to meet our needs. Thus prayer begins with a sudden expression of anguish or sorrow, of anger or joy. Raw life experience drives us to cry out from the depths of despair, from the pinnacles of ecstasy; even our most sophisticated prayers have their origin here. Nor ought it be otherwise. Spiritual pilgrims do not seek to avert the outcry, but instead strive to align self-centeredness with Yahweh's might, majesty, dominion, and power.

Repentance is the final goal of prayer.

Six months ago the eternal flame of the oil fields sputtered and died. Yesterday his wife left. Now, with bright orange sunlight pouring through windows closed against the southern heat, it seems to him that he is already running, fighting back sleep and the hostile night, heading for Detroit again. He closes the door behind him; he begins nailing boards over the windows. All around are neighbors watching the solemn entombment in curiously ordered silence. His tired, slow hammering clatters and echoes away against sidewalks and walls and trees until at last each window of the small house is utterly blank, sightless. Then he stoops down and takes in his arms an awkward-looking bundle that appears to be a homemade knapsack. To the silent street he says: "Tell the mortgage company they can have it now. They can have it all." Then, walking past the neighbors and the many other boarded-up houses, he says: "Well, I reckon that's it, folks. Yes, I reckon that's it, by God." And louder he says: "Headin' back up north. Ain't nothing left here anyway. I figure it's about time I went home." A fresh wind comes up suddenly; he feels cleansed, refreshed.

It is not creation that changes. Rather, the one who prays is bent in God's direction. We shall/can never bend Yahweh to our direction. (The Holy and Terrible One knows every need, is aware of the sparrow's falling.) Human beings shriek in the face of the way things are; we shout to Yahweh as if we were the first creatures to ever feel pain. But we are not the first: the ancient witness echoes in our ears as we stand, vulnerable and afraid and wrong, standing in the need of prayer. And prayer is not wishful thinking, nor does it end with outcry. Whether petition or praise, our prayers are informed by the past. The entire sweep of holy history becomes part of the individual's reaching out. We are not the first to shriek, and we are not the first to have denied Christ. The Word of the Lord: You shall have no other gods before me.

Three times over Jesus says that which breaks the heart and frees the spirit of Simon Peter: Feed my sheep.

In the beginning was the Word, and the Word was with God, and the Word was God. Ongoing creation spins a web of mystery around those who dare to pray. Prayer is the double-edged sword (our weapon, God's weapon) that cuts to the core of human clay.

By remembrance and rehearsal of past events, prayer advances. We testify to divine self-disclosure in our own lives and in the lives of those who have gone before. Our prayers are offered to the Transcendent One on behalf of all creation. We cry out for the sake of the brain-dead child who cannot speak. Within each of us breathes everyone who ever was and everyone who ever will be. As we finally grasp the truth of this, repentance begins. Through correlation of ancient witness with present historical occurrence, the Word becomes living encounter: We are free to live, to follow the

Fiddler on the Roof, to announce the acceptable year of the Lord.

We are undoomed, living within the fluid, unpredictable matrix of events that forms the peculiar medium of divine response. Human beings are special subjects of Yahweh's judgment/love: curious, recalcitrant, inventive creatures bound to the authority of Almighty God, who makes use of every random, imperfect, sinful human effort unto the fulfillment of holy purpose.

And all along the tattered and costly way, creation is being shaped and veered and set free by the instrumentality of lucid, vulnerable Spirit people, who have finally given up trying to be God. They have ceased believing in dogma; they have stepped onto the tightrope of passionate commitment to Yahweh.

Decisions made in this present validate or invalidate all that has gone before, make possible or impossible all that is yet to come. Breathless, expectant, the entire created universe has been awaiting this moment. Each human life is of absolute significance; the least human act is sanctified in the vector of God's high time. Divine meaning, magnitude, and direction cannot be discerned by finite creatures. But God's purpose will not be thwarted. The doors to salvation have been thrown open wide. We can curse God, create hell, deepen separation, but we are not able to divert the course of redemption.

No human action can cancel out covenant.

2

We tremble before the mystery of the stubborn, unfrail Word that can be neither fully understood nor successfully ignored. Each of us is a separate being, simultaneously bound to this island planet and part of spiderlike star formations moving outward in space 500 million light years away. We live and die as dream-creatures wandering lonely between spiraling galaxies and utter Earth-dependence. Yet as people of the story we proclaim to all creation that our God is a living God whose Word sustains, whose incarnation reveals inchoate redemption, whose death/resurrection cruciformity accomplishes salvation in this present-yet-to-be.

Take nothing for your journey, no staff, nor bag, nor bread, nor money.

The pilgrim people of God live under the sign of the Cross. In the faithfulness of Christ was revealed unconditional promise (fully God) and obedience (fully man). The Christ event was unique, once-for-all, sufficient. Yet by *anamnesis* (standing present to a past event through corporate remembrance), we bear witness to the saving action of God-in-Christ. Although everyone is born into separation and is unable to escape the state of sin that corrupts knowledge as well as action, nevertheless, each of our lives has been *worded* by the Holy One to be of inestimable value. We have been turned and re-turned by Yahweh's rainbow mercy. It is sin that divides creation from itself. But Yahweh has broken the power of sin. The *power* of sin is broken. Yet earthly battles tear at faith, the devil whispers seductive truth designed to crush the spirit; these are interim times. Too much information about global problems and national failings assaults us, encouraging retreat into apathy. The fierce attack of God is unleashed on every emotional numbness: whatever has been constructed as protection against holy insecurity is beseiged. Unutterable groanings find expression when existence-bound creatures come up against the personal, animal-like, Totally Other, Transcendent One. The way of the story drives us to prayer (shriek/remembrance/repentance). The Word of the Lord: Take your son, your only son Isaac, whom you love, and go to the land of Moriah, and offer him there as a burnt offering upon one of the mountains of which I shall tell you.

My Father, if it is possible, let this cup pass from me; nevertheless, not as I will, but as thou wilt.

The disciples received from Jesus neither creed nor code. Rather, they were made recipients of the event called resurrection; they bore common witness to God's historical incarnation/resurrection. The Christ event precipitated a faith community of frightened, doubting, Spirit-filled men and women. And the faith community understood itself as an extension of the body of Christ, a concrete visible sign to the world of Yahweh's glorious destiny come at last: a sacramental body gathered to manifest and make Eucharist as those representationally responsible for all time, all space. This pilgrim people hammered out specific forms of worship (liturgy). But the particular forms were always subservient to the crucial witness—standing present to the mighty acts of God in history and to the culmination of divine revelation in Jesus Christ. Day after day, week after week, the people came together to do liturgy, to celebrate Christ and him crucified, to re-member the body of Christ on behalf of creation.

It begins with confession. It begins with acknowledging that the world has dragged us down, the world has prevailed once again. We are scarred by sin, ensnared by demons. That is our confession. And the proclamation is this: Jesus Christ lived and died and was raised from the dead. We are the redeemed of Christ who bear the burden of God's radical freedom—Spirit people broken and sustained. The Word is spoken in our midst; it is thrown at us like a stone. By *anamnesis,* past event (salvation history) becomes present reality. By means of remembrance, the church celebrates resurrection-presence. Scriptural witness and the Word of God place us in vertical time-space identity: then and now, there and here.

The gospel proclaims God in our midst dancing because sin is overcome, shouting because death is no more. Yahweh is victorious warrior-animal: God's triumphant covenant-love is greater than sin, greater than death, greater than fear of death. The Lord of Hosts is near at hand. We are wanderers in the wilderness, delivered out of the land of Egypt, fed by the Holy One. We have been washed in the waters of the Flood, cleansed by the River Jordan, baptized with Christ into everlasting hope. Jesus did not preach gospel; he *was* gospel.

The good news is that no one is expendable.

And the task of preaching the good news belongs to the new community. But it is not enough to proclaim the Word within the *ecclesia* (the church). Yahweh-Spirit-Christ calls us beyond confession and celebration, shoves us back into the world again to live the third great act of worship: offering. The implication of Christian hope is mission. Enabled by grace, we carry the Word to every last woman, man, and child on the face of the Earth. We carry the Word back into the world that has beaten us down. And there is more. More is reserved for us: the free and total offering of tenuous life (shadowy death) on behalf of Wholly Other. Confession leads to proclamation; proclamation begets missional intentionality. We are a servant people charged with telling the story to individual human beings everywhere—whether or not the story has been heard before, whether or not the individual believes anything, whether or not the person can even hear the words we speak.

By means of vertical time-space identity (high time), the Resurrected Christ is present with us today. And in Eucharist, basic elements of existence are sanctified, offered back to the community of resurrection so that we might yet be sustained and renewed who are nothing but ashes and dust. It is in dying that we live, not only in final death but also in that daily giving up of illusion which constitutes obedience to Redeemer God.

You are the salt of the earth; but if salt has lost its taste, how shall its saltness be restored?

The solitary decision of the Spirit person is a deadly serious matter: it is dedication of life-journey to intentional, dangerous vulnerability. In our time the commitment may involve dragging the church back to its original self-understanding. For Rosa Parks it meant challenging segregationist authorities. They say for Peter it included returning to Rome to be crucified. Many struggle for justice and freedom and peace, working outside the historical church. Their efforts too are shaped into Yahweh's salvation vector.

*I was hungry and you gave me food, I was thirsty and you gave me drink,
I was a stranger and you welcomed me, I was naked and you clothed me,
I was sick and you visited me, I was in prison and you came to me.*

Those who have decided in favor of life and who battle
with the principalities and powers of this world are salvation
colleagues in completed-yet-not-completed redemption.
And redemption colleagues are in eternal conflict with those
who daily choose to close down the future, to neutralize the
world. In every part of Earth people have been dehuman-
ized, categorized, labeled. Whenever we place a derogatory
or subhuman name on living human beings, those persons,
for us, cease to live. A homeless man is transformed into an
object of scorn by those who call him derelict, bum. Powers
of divisiveness invade schools and churches and halls of
justice. In an African nation the white minority pursues a
course of racial separation, confident that the world's need
for certain valuable minerals will outweigh international
outrage. But Spirit people throughout the world will not
surrender the battle against racism, against economic imperialism, against disenfranchisement. These are they who
continually read the signs of the times in the light of God's
continuing revelation. Many are outspokenly prophetic;
others work backstage, moving silently to rearrange sets and
effect subtle shadings of red-blue-amber light.

Jesus was God's Messiah; he commissioned those who
remained (the remnant pilgrim community) to take up messianic mission.

Upon us has fallen the mantle of Elijah. The Man for Others is Lord. And he is calling us to faithfully exercise his min-

istry. In these intervening times we are called to respond in freedom, to be agents (on Earth) of Yahweh's unearthly purpose. As messianic ones we exorcise demons and announce resurrection-faith while recognizing that the church itself has become a corrupt bastion of comfort, a supporter of *status quo.* Missional response is solitary, unpopular, based on the unseen, substantiated by no*thing.* Spirit people are humble before God, not before human beings. Modern prophets dare to walk into the presence of dictators and terrorists, bishops and prime ministers, announcing the Word, interpreting present events, claiming divine authority.

History is being created and shaped each day.

3

And the Lord God is stalking the land because we have ravaged that which was entrusted to us. Judgment hovers over military councils, corporation boards, and terrorist organizations. That which was intended for good has become an invisible arrow pointed at the heart of humankind. The devil has a plan for our lives. And time is running in the devil's favor, running past us with grim fury, crashing over concrete walls of apathy and beyond into the River.

Before we can formulate answers, the questions are obsolete.

We have become fugitives. In these interim days a gradual sculpting of personal identity is too costly; we must decide the future. It is the God-ordained task of our generation to bring healing (this-worldly salvation) to shackled Earth— even though we are strangers in a culture heaving and buckling with change. We are worn down by the gray drizzle of bureaucracy. Many have simply ceased to respond. And the powerful ones feed upon our apathy, using it to further encroach on individual liberties.

Evil personified is confronting us in the wilderness. And the temptation is to give up, to leave problems with the next generation, to let our eyes go vacant. But the next generation is bombarded with fatalistic predictions, thrust into varieties of emotional detachment.

Individual effort can change the course of the world.

The early resurrection community stands before us, holding a mirror that we might see ourselves reflected in the historic corridor of faith sacrifice. Reflected there are souls from every generation who created the future on behalf of the whole world. The courage of Karen Silkwood adjoins the intentionality of Cesar Chávez and links up with the vision of Albert Einstein, which reaches out to the commitment of Martin Luther King, Jr. And new prophets are even now rising up to search out centers of power and reveal myriad deceptions that heretofore have gone unchallenged.

Those who offer their lives messianically take the risk that the tides of history will sweep away all of their accomplishments. But in reality, the gift of freely given death will enable the birth of a new future; nothing created is lost to Yahweh. Spirit people are out of joint with society. When others counsel caution, they proceed.

Each day people are victimized, then blamed for being victims. With the eyes of resurrection-consciousness, Spirit people recognize that information gathering is often no more than a diversionary tactic; page follows page of statistical research while life fades from the skeletons of a famine-wasted people. We will never know whether or not what we do is right. Faith is the assurance of things hoped for, the conviction of things not seen. Yahweh has commissioned us to bring our own people out of Egypt. And this is the year of the Lord's demand.

In North Carolina, Hispanic families live in migrant worker camps where there are no windowscreens or toilets, where bloodstains on the floor bear silent witness to the hard fact that many doctors refuse to treat these workers. In New York City violent beatings and muggings have become an expected part of life. A Vietnam veteran takes his own life in front of a belatedly erected monument to that war. Auto workers discover that the industrial midwest is crumbling, eroding, becoming a new dust bowl.

But resurrection hope boldly proclaims that which is radically new in history.

Based on remembrance of God's historical ingression, faith announces: It is not necessary for the world to be unfed; the church can be healed of its fragmentation; structures of justice can be designed and implemented; nuclear holocaust is not inevitable. In the quiet breathing of a spring-awakened forest, possibility can be heard unfolding. The untamed potential of ongoing creation will emerge through the instrumentality of Spirit people who are themselves lonely and afraid. The territory of expectation teems with life; it is turbulent with unending travail and full-tilt commitment. And being a teller of the story carries intrinsically neither reward nor recognition. More will be demanded than we had planned to give; we will shrink from death. But the faith community will not stop. The people will tell the story in spite of brutality and dogs and electronic surveillance, in spite of bombings and assassinations and every kind of oppression. We are part of a great cloud of witnesses who have faced the same solitude, the same evil.

In this fleeting moment we can reverse the catastrophic progress of nuclear suicide. It is up to the intentional, messianic ones to structure the future as colleagues of God. On behalf of Yahweh we are witnesses to hope, attesting to the ultimate salvation of everything that is. This generation must hear anew the story of the Holy One, who sustains the complex, tenuous web of life and who mourns human greed and destructiveness.

At one time or another, each of us believes it is possible to keep life contained. That somehow we can emerge unscarred. Surely we can navigate from this shore to the next without expending life's blood upon the sand. But wholeness (holiness) does not consist in being perfect or untouched by the ravages of the world. And life is not fair. The guilty go free; the innocent suffer. And the ways of God are not fair: the door to salvation is open to all. Mystery abounds. Sooner or later each of us will be torn apart by the world. The only question is: In what cause, on whose behalf, will life's blood be expended?

4

Unprotected from those who work evil, scattered and purged by Yahweh, we live as nomads in the service of the Lord.

A fugitive people is the resurrection community. We continue in spite of the magnitude, the impossibility, of the task, looking ahead to ultimate transformation and fulfillment of history. Jesus appointed twelve to be with him and to be sent out to preach and have authority to cast out demons. Representationally responsible, acting on behalf of Israel fallen, the disciples who gathered after resurrection formed the nucleus of a new Israel; they were apostles, messengers, no longer twelve. And the messianic community developed various forms of liturgical worship that the corporate body might recall the life, death, and resurrection of Jesus Christ. Further, worship provided ongoing sustenance to individual members of the body of Christ for daily life-struggle. The various liturgical forms were means to an end—never important in themselves. By incarnation/resurrection Yahweh tore down every barrier between the sacred and the secular, between worship and daily living. No place is without Christ's presence; rite and ceremony must flow out of total life-offering made to the Mysterious Creator by humble, obedient creatures.

The earliest apostles lived in immediate expectation of end times: they believed that the glorious, total Easter Day disclosure would soon be followed by apocalyptic kingdom. And in truth, the first signs of the kingdom (Yahweh's initiative in shattering the power of evil) had been established.

But the *eschaton* (end times) did not arrive. The Lord did not return. What happened was *not* what was expected. What happened was this: we were delivered from darkness and transferred into high time.

The golden hoop that the teacher wears in her nose glitters with noon sun. She is leading a group of children in simple, lyrical songs; beneath bare feet is soft, warm dust. Behind them stands a mud hut. Where maharajas long ago hunted tiger and wild boar, villagers now learn to read and write. The teacher smiles at the little cluster of children. She tells a story about how once she had raised chickens and sold eggs. Because she could not read, she was cheated by the egg collector, thereby losing all of her property. Low, dense mountains surround that inchoate classroom and the village and a hundred other villages from which arise the intentional, persistent voices of people who are teaching and being taught, of people hoping and learning to hope.

Our mission is to be a servant people, embedded in history, burning with a vision that sees beyond the unmapped, soaring span of earth-duration.

End time is not fully accomplished yet; we have not reached the goal. It remains for us to take seriously this present, drawing comfort from holy history, shaping the future. But we are not miracle workers. And Jesus was not a miracle worker either, or preacher or teacher or prophet, though he manifested all of these: Incarnate Other pushed at the borders of human/divine encounter. And today Christ Jesus lives, driving us on toward radical obedience. In obedience does the church go about its manifold tasks—preaching, prophecy, teaching, healing. But the central ministry of the resurrection community is to rejoice in the midst of suffering, to take unto ourselves the dying of the world. And in celebrating brokenness we bear the marks of Jesus' crucifixion. And in bearing those marks we also share in redemption prefigured through the revelation of God Almighty (Alleluia!) in the historical event called resurrection.

5

Perhaps he had seen too many executions. Perhaps that night the glaring prison lights had burned into the quiet isolation of his mind. The onlookers—by special invitation only—sat rigid, unbreathing. It was always so. But he, with invulnerable calm, watched the prisoner, his own mortality floating somewhere northwest of the red brick penitentiary and far above mortal time. The violence in the room did not fascinate or appall him. Yet something caused his eyes to flicker at the last instant before death rushed upon the prisoner. An instant's flicker, so brief as to be doubted. It was as if a hand had reached out and closed his eyes, then opened them again, and he not knowing why. But Saul, still breathing threats and murder against the disciples of the Lord, went to the high priest and asked him for letters to the synagogues at Damascus, so that if he found any belonging to the Way, men or women, he might bring them bound to Jerusalem. Now as he journeyed he approached Damascus, and suddenly a light from heaven flashed about him.

Theology is a matter of life and death.

Theologians are not dabblers; commitment to God is a prerequisite of their task. Nevertheless, all dogma, every systematic understanding of human encounter with the Infinite, remains provisional, partial, open to debate. And although the basic proclamation of faith does not change, interpretation (doctrine) must continually be revised in order to communicate adequately with each successive generation. Theology attempts to chart life experience. It does not reveal truth; it draws out the implications of original witness. We proclaim gospel, then offer explanations as to what the story means for us in this space-time. But faithful followers of Yahweh Sabaoth travel with very little baggage; no interpretation is written in stone; no single theology is correct. In every new age the work of theological explanation must recommence.

There are no road maps to guide us; we have entered a pathless region, a wild land filled with multitudinous choices. But the wilderness itself, and each individual life within it, is sustained by redemption-promise: The momentum of God is building and building unto final fulfillment.

The chronological curtain that was sundered on Good Friday cannot be mended. Measured time holds little importance for our lives. Satan uses clocks (moving in arbitrary cadence) as a means of distracting us from unmitigated commitment to the Unsynonymous. But in Yahweh's desert, shadows soften the lines dividing the seasons of life; there is no set path, only a steep ascent that is never the same for any two travelers. Most accurately, *anno Domini* is the year that *belongs* to our Lord.

St. Paul was always God's man. He was not converted to belief in Yahweh when the flash of stark light cut and dived into his consciousness, stopping him blind. What was transformed (expanded) was his understanding of Yahweh's revelation. Before even Ananias came with the Word of grace and the scales fell from Paul's eyes, repentance had begun. The persecutor became one with the persecuted.

Each of us carries around a bundle of assumptions.

The answers we received as children—before the questions could be formulated—confine us, lock us into a borrowed universe. Someone else's system organizes early life experience into *shalls* and *shoulds* and *shall nots.* Then, in time, Totally Other breaks in, rearranging our world so that we stumble over the old ideas. Yahweh destroys the pillars supporting everything we hold to be self-evident. We call out for parents and they are not there; we look to our leaders and they cannot help. When we have been seized by God, struck blind by the Holy One, intellectual constructs fall. At the instant of crisis, knowing goes beyond thinking, and there is sudden apprehension of Mystery. Later, perhaps, rationality will reflect on the encounter. But the transforming moment simply *is.* And the Almighty offers no explanations. God seeks us out at unlikely times and places, sends us on unthinkable missions: "Rise up and go to the street called Straight, and inquire in the house of Judas for a man of Tarsus named Saul."

Within the earthly realm, spirituality is manifested primarily through suffering. In creatureliness (by presenting ourselves daily, dying to illusion) do we show forth the Spirit. People who endure and hope and celebrate and decide are the earthen vessels whom God chooses to fill with spiritual treasure. We are afflicted in every way, but not crushed; perplexed, but not driven to despair; persecuted, but not forsaken; struck down, but not destroyed. For while we live we are always being given up to death for Jesus' sake, so that the life of Jesus may be manifested in our mortal flesh. This is God's creation: no other world has been given us. And the mortal world necessarily involves suffering. But by resurrection of Jesus Christ did Yahweh sanctify the human condition. Finitude served as vehicle for divine revelation. And incarnation/resurrection became the basis for endurance, the basis for celebration, the foundation of hope.

Spirituality does not set a person apart; it does not transcend the conditions of existence. For us there is no transcendence into a domain-beyond-domains where suffering disappears. Therefore, the spiritual one is always a person among persons. This person wakes up crying in the morning. Smokes too much. Visits a dying woman weekly and is afraid. Recently had shock therapy. Can't spell. Failed in business. Just had a pacemaker attached. Was raped. Tried to commit suicide. Is confined to a wheelchair for life. Knows he is one drink away from being drunk for a year. Doesn't understand the sermons at church. Used to be a doctor. Flunked out of school. Doesn't know who her father is.

The Spirit manifests through people embroiled in the world, people who hope against hope. Earthbound vessels all, not transcendent, not despairing. Thus, we present ourselves before the Source of life as broken, sinful people, celebrating the Power that raised Jesus Christ from the dead and that lifts up each individual's suffering.

We do not lose heart. Though we are wasting away, yet shall we be renewed by the Giver of life.

The way of the story is not tragic, in spite of the tragedy we witness. It is not dolorous, in spite of the grief we experience. Explosive grace brings kinetic redemption into this present, a foretaste of what is yet to be, all-pervasive and everywhere alive. Beyond happiness and even joy is grace. The strange truth of it is that we cannot know light without darkness, grace without sin, nor can we fully know life until we have known death. But by faith the covenant people proclaim Yahweh triumphant. The entire creation is homeward bound. The kingdom will come. In all power and glory and majesty. Forever and ever. Amen.

6

"I wish I was wearing a necktie and looking like Montgomery Clift—before the accident—so that things would go well for me. It feels like the years are set in concrete with me tied forever to one end of the slab, forever until they lower my dead body into the ground. I tell you, Charlie, there's a special hell reserved for me if God is all gray and righteous." His breathing rasped across the inviolable, cool space. An air conditioner hummed, and outside the sun was setting full orange.

Nobody knows just what to do. Everyone is stumped. We lock the front and back doors against intruders, but fear gets in. Abruptly born, tentatively held together with half-truths and fantasies, we huddle against the driving force of death. Spirit-journey progresses despite the hard fact that no instruction book was ever provided. Multiple theories and plans arise, each claiming to make sense of life. At best they are provisional, partial insights, quickly codified by fallible human beings who are hungry for solutions. Movements, cults, organizations stand in readiness to enroll those who crave serenity. But spirit-journey cannot be translated into manageable, predictable terms. What of the woman who practices law with a fierce passion, knowing that her cancer, now in remission, could return any day? Or the man entering life outside a mental hospital for the first time in ten years? Or the family sleeping five to a bed? No earthly plan or program will suffice when we have crossed over into the amazed shadow-region where human finitude leaves off and Mystery begins.

All dogma is provisional—often helpful, but never ultimate.

The One who made the world and everything in it, being Lord of heaven and earth, does not live in shrines made by human hands. Yahweh is not contained in creed or theology or sacrament. The Word we proclaim bursts the confines of every institution. Thus, Christian community finds itself caught between uncontainable Other and human yearning for definable structure. The Holy One breaks in pieces the temples dedicated to religion. Tellers of the story hold myriad opinions. Perhaps they have only one thing in common: proclaiming the enabling Word that endures and sustains and burns outward beyond time. The gospel frees us to celebrate this diversity within the faith-community. Engaged in unidirectional enterprise, we are finite messengers on an infinite mission. And Yahweh will transform the diverse strands of testimony into swirling, luminescent single-glory.

A voice cries: And as I prophesied, there was a noise, and behold, a rattling; and the bones came together, bone to its bone. We work and pray and proclaim in service of the same Lord. Each believer is called to strive for the coming of God's kingdom, working alongside others (whether or not they are likable or intelligent or popular) who comprise the body of Christ. We are driven to stand present to the wonderful mystery of each human being. And Yahweh, working through historical reality, pierces the knowing that is not-knowing, replaces anguish with hope, terror with joy. The God-given Word of life: Go forth, tell everyone what was told to you. Human life is of inestimable value.

Do not be afraid.

The people of God gather regularly to confess, to proclaim, and to offer. Worship makes explicit the implicit basis of faith: through Word and sacrament the body rehearses holy history. Our dull ears are opened. The church's liturgy employs powerful methods in its efforts to strengthen us, the frail messengers who carry gospel to the outermost reaches of earthly space. And liturgy penetrates the barrier between conscious and unconscious mind. Repetitive, patient, incessant, it leaves an indelible mark upon the fabric of our lives. Alleluias tumble across the centuries. A great cloud of witnesses calls forth the response of total being. The Word is announced in an environment which can accommodate all the manifold and terrific complex of human experience that is contained within the pilgrim community. Liturgy invites us to full participation, we who are drenched in sin and utterly unworthy. (If we wait to partake of the holy mysteries until worthiness is attained, we will never come to God's table.) Worship is corporate rededication to the way of the Cross.

Our sins are forgiven; new creation is now. Enabled by grace, we present ourselves in thankfulness, with humility. Then we are in motion again, on the run, hurrying to outrun the devil. This week we shall yet again offer our lives to Ultimate Mystery. And Yahweh will take the composite offering and forge the deed of God: the vector of divine purpose headed straightaway for wild, unbridled divine salvation.

The darkness is passing away, and the true light is already shining.

No, of course, it isn't safe. Spirit-journey will never be safe. It begins with elemental, troubling, gnawing questions within a maze of inherited answers. Later, as wonder gives way to fatigue, questions increase; cracks begin to show in the enamel of secondhand solutions. There is absurdity beneath the spectacle of human existence. But out of absurdity comes awareness of suffering, of dependence upon the Unsynonymous One. Profound, inexplicable Mystery becomes the only source of strength, integration. To be overwhelmed by (not mystically one with) the Eternal is breathtaking, breath-giving. The prideful struggle to attain certainty is relinquished, replaced with Spirit-consciousness, born in the solitude of desert autumn.

The messianic life-style is not oriented to success. In earthly terms, we must lose everything. And good works do not buy God's favor. Nor can we manipulate Yahweh to do our will. To follow Christ is to take up the Cross, to suffer in the midst of a broken world, rejoicing in the hope of the Spirit, proclaiming resurrection gospel. Over the span of centuries, men and women of faith have chosen sharply contrasting life-styles. The commonality is expanded awareness: these tellers of the story see the holy in all life; they perceive creation as interdependent unity—what harms one life harms every life. Thus the borders of the universe are seen to encompass the spiritual journey even of the one who obtains food from garbage cans, the runaway who panhandles for change, the executive struggling with alcoholism, or the man on a city sidewalk carrying a sandwich board that reads: "I am blind and you can see. Please don't pass me by." O how the human spirit longs for something unconditional! And while we are thrashing (while we are yet denying God and the Christ and the spirit-journey), we nevertheless yearn for something Ultimate, hoping against hope that the final word will not be emptiness and fate and death.

It happens to all of God's children; it happens that memories come back with a kind of vengeance: And they will not be denied. Sin weighs us down with all of the things we have done and the things we have left undone. Make no mistake, even a child knows that this year is not like last year. The child says, "It isn't the same," and that's right. It can never be the same.

Asleep in the front seat, the small boy did not feel the automobile sliding across dark pavement. But he heard his mother scream when the car fled the ground and tilted violently downward. Next there were branches scraping, tearing at the windows and doors of the rapidly moving vehicle. Then the crash. For several minutes he did not realize it had been a single, huge pine tree that had jolted them with such violence. "Mom!" he said, "Mommmm!" while fearful darkness closed in around him. She answered; her voice sounded thin, small: "I'm here. I'm here. But I can't move, honey. Oh God, I can't move." Then he saw where she was lying crumpled under the dashboard. Outside, all wild and sad, an owl screeched across the night. The boy acted without thinking. He spoke some words to his mother, then crawled out of the car window and jumped down onto a cushion of twigs and needles and snow that massed under the silent pine tree. Directly away from the car he walked, slipping on patches of dark ice, clambering up the harsh embankment. When he reached the road, he began walking fast. Not a single car passed him. He went on, walking faster and faster. Until finally, up ahead, he saw the lights of a house flash on, and he began to run. Startled as they were entering their house, a man and a woman saw the small boy come flying out of the night, scrambling and yelling and stumbling. "Help me!" he yelled. "My mom needs help; she's hurt! And I . . . I'm afraid of the dark!"

We are moving together in mysterious progression, moving from inexplicable *here* to destined, glorious *there.*

A disc jockey in Detroit was on the air late one Christmas Eve, when the only people listening were the people who needed the radio for company. No one else was talking to those people right then. He was the only one out there for them, the ones who were in agony, or afraid of the dark, or just plain lost in Earth-time. And each one carrying a sandwich board: Please don't pass me by. Maybe what the disc jockey said that night made all the difference. Maybe his *yes* or *no* opened or shut something deep within the hearts of those forgotten ones who waited by the radio, expecting a miracle.

Mary stood weeping outside the tomb, and as she wept she stooped to look into the tomb, and she saw two angels in white sitting where the body of Jesus had lain, one at the head and one at the feet. They said to her, "Woman, why are you weeping?" She said to them, "Because they have taken away my Lord, and I do not know where they have laid him." Saying this, she turned round and saw Jesus standing, but she did not know that it was Jesus.

7

It is very late, with time flowing around us like a brook divided by an outcrop of jagged rocks. We have fallen away —the community has fallen away from the mission. Politicians and business leaders have tried to make the church into just one more predictable, usable institution. But the story is still being told; nothing can silence or tame the story. On behalf of humankind, Christ Jesus commissioned us to dream, to grope beyond ourselves, beyond space and time, to reach out for the impossible. In the eyes of the world, Christ's gospel is offensive. It dreams too large a dream: grace is extended to all as a free gift, undeserved. If we take the ancient witness seriously, we can no longer stand on our own two feet. Utter God-dependence and no-strings-attached grace: these offend and shock. The call to repentance means giving up everything. Full-tilt commitment to Yahweh threatens idolatry. And often we don't want God intruding on the security of possessions or on comfortable self-pity. No. As proclaimers we will be resisted. As prophets we will be ostracized, sawn in half. Even within ourselves there is conflict between the demons and Spirit freedom.

How can we believe what we have not seen? Because seeing is not the same thing as believing. Faith is not a matter of logical implication. It is rooted in historical experience. But the leap from history to eternal dimension requires courageous decision on the part of individual human creatures. (What a glorious decision—to *believe* what we have not seen or touched, to see with the eyes of faith what was always there!) Yet because we are frail, we also continue to doubt. Only fanaticism would reject the ongoing nature of doubt; it is a necessary component of passionate belief. But God will not let us go; Yahweh has hold of creation (struggling, lost and frightened, believing and doubting), and God will never let go. Through historical event, through sacrament and preaching, the Holy One speaks to us. The Word addresses heart and mind, reaching into the deeps until even atomic structure trembles with God-encounter. When the story has reached our core, we can never be the same again.

Through the deepest valley on earth the Jordan curves and twists. And we have been baptized in the waters of Jordan to the end of urgent gospel proclamation. There is an insistence, a kind of haste, about the proclamation. The demand is to travel light, to divest ourselves of staff, bread, money. Corporate worship serves as a way station through which we must pass quickly, taking sustenance for our journey to the mountain of God. Eucharist is not meant to be a service of contemplation: we are a people on the move, with chronological time running out; the re-membered body gathers, then disperses into the world. Again God drives us back into severe, painful opposition. We who have heard the Word and who have been fertile ground for the seed of gospel announcement—we have been commissioned.

It is not only the forces of antagonism that we face, but also our own unwillingness to live with holy insecurity.

When we become anxious and worried, we reach for something to hang on to—food, cigarettes, alcohol, drugs. The temptation is to revert to the structures of childhood. (The idolatry of childhood is an imagined security wherein we are allowed to curl up in the back seat of the family car while our parents make the decisions.) Reality is too harsh; we want the world to become a magical place, a lustrous fantasy. And Satan purports to offer all of that. But Satan is a liar; nothing in the world will fill the emptiness. The power (control) we seek will not satisfy. Nor can drugs transform reality. Idol worship is always backward movement. Turn away, says the Lord God. Turn away from your idols and step forward into new creation.

Every burden has been lifted. Hear the Word of God: It isn't the end of the world if you never finished school. Don't let the past prevent you from taking the risk of messianic commitment. A voice cries: Will you be doers of the Word and not hearers only? Will you live out in your lives the crucified Lord, will you proclaim Jesus Christ and him crucified? You can change the course of history. Individual decisionality can prevent the pending disasters of this present. Today the world is on the brink of chaos; we are being torn apart by a series of seemingly unrelated economic, social, and political crises. The entire planet shudders under the judgment of Yahweh. But its future rests partly in our hands. We can break the cycle of catastrophe; we can open our ears to the Word. For lo, these many years have we waited for a leader. The people cry out: We are bereft of leaders! Thus says Yahweh: I, I am the Lord, and besides me there is no savior. Behold, I am doing a new thing; now it springs forth, do you not perceive it?

Can't you see it? The prophetic Word is gathering, tumbling, flourishing; insignificant places are giving birth to the messianic. The famous are using their fame to challenge the mighty. On street corners the Word of affirmation is spoken. Can't you see it happening? The remnant people are alive and proclaiming and reaching out. (You say it isn't possible; you're afraid in your heart that it's too late for us; born too late, you think.) By the power of God it's not too late. It's not impossible. This is our moment to tell the story; it is a single, glinting moment, but it is enough. And in Jesus Christ, the One who was tempted in every way as we are yet who did not succumb to the devil, we see new creation moving forward. Yahweh is reaching into our personal histories and bringing us back to life in order that we might know the Shepherd. Thus says the Lord: I myself will search for my sheep, and will seek them out. And I will rescue them from all places where they have been scattered on a day of clouds and thick darkness.

We have been rescued from alienation, from loneliness, from estrangement, and from every brokenhearted moment. We have been snatched away from confusion and sickness and ignorance and temerity.

The remnant people are deciding that it is not too late. They are risking everything; they have counted the cost and discovered that the cost is too high, but they are going forward anyway, driven by the Spirit, prodded by Yahweh, sustained by Christ Jesus. Can't you see it now? Can't you feel the motion of the universe? From forbidden sacramental enclaves behind the Iron Curtain the enabling Word is proclaimed. In the region of Philadelphia a young boy is keeping watch over the homeless. And a message goes forth from London that the hungry shall be fed. From South Africa and Poland comes the announcement: Be not afraid; for behold, I bring you good news of a great joy that will come to all the people. God-in-Christ has breathed life into the remnant that they might live and know the Lord and announce to all creation: What is scattered will be gathered together; what is torn asunder will be healed; every valley shall be lifted up and every mountain and hill be made low.

The grass withers, the flower fades; but the Word of our God will stand forever.

VI. Interloper from Beyond

And on that day there shall be inscribed on the bells of the horses, "Holy to the Lord."

—ZECHARIAH 14:20

1

Blessed be the Triune One who has blessed us in Christ with every spiritual (enlivening, empowering) blessing in the heavenly places, even as Yahweh chose us in Christ before the foundations of the world, that we should be holy and blameless before God. For by grace have we been saved through faithfulness; and this is not our own doing but the gift of Yahweh—not because of works, lest any should boast.

God never did give up.

No, it was not that. In spatial, atemporal terms history *is* present encounter with God-in-Christ: the time of conflict is now; the time of Christ's victory is now. Creation is the eternal work of Redeemer God, who was and is and is to come. And creation is always now, new-emergent, never before, leap-or-else, momentous. But we just never know what's next because things keep changing, because redemption is what God-in-Christ *does* in eternal, eschatological (final) immediacy, transforming human life, uplifting all things created, in and to the glory of Wholly Other, Unsynonymous God. We never know what's next at all, who have come such a long way up slow out of the waters of baptism and fighting to keep from drowning and almost drowning anyway, in spite of the calling, yet refusing to stop because of it. We can't stop and won't stop. But it's a hard business to stand under God's faithfulness; it's hard. All the while doubting that light can and will shine forth from the darkness of our own dark hearts; believing the Paul of 2 Corinthians and all the while doubting ourselves; not the call but the self doubting, and in the dark crying still, lost and alone in the glory of it, crying. Yes, that's how the song must end and begin and end again. Triumphant and sad, dying away. Marching up the sky, singing with Joan of Arc, singing the one song and preaching that Yahweh is the all-consuming fire. It is God who consumes all. Amen.

The devil is tempting us every day and every hour to deny Christ.

But Yahweh is not finite; the Lord is not limited by any principle whatsoever. Let the devil scream, God says. The One who rides through the desert has spoken: I am God, not man. Let the devil scream. And in every present, every now, we are up against, surrounded by, the holy—caught between God and God. Therein is Christ King (Alleluia!); Lord Jesus Christ is King, who is alive today and living and shattering and everywhere changing, turning, creating anew— the new wine of God tearing apart the old wineskins of understanding, of doctrine. A voice cries: From this time forth I make you hear new things, hidden things which you have not known.

Is a lamp brought in to be put under a bushel, or under a bed, and not on a stand? For there is nothing hid, except/to be made manifest; nor is anything secret, except to come to light.

And the day is coming when the Earth shall see the east wind, the wind of the Lord, proceeding from the wilderness (as instantaneous and complete as all silence), and the Earth shall rise up to gaze upon that dawning articulation of scentless flowers and irrevocable destination found; the Earth shall rise up. As the Lord God knows everything that needs to be known and is ever present where the Holy Presence is needed, so shall the day unfold when the Son of Man is seated at the right hand of power, riding on the clouds of heaven. And we who are united with him in death shall surely be united with him in that final resurrection: For the law of the Spirit of life in Christ Jesus has set me free from the law of sin and death. And I consider that the sufferings of this present time are not worth comparing with the glory that is to be revealed in us.

Behold, now is the acceptable time; behold, now is the day of salvation.

Thus spirit-journey continues on: on the run and stubborn and brandishing radiant gospel, carrying the Word, coming dark along the Earth, trailing wondrous joy across the dead of night. Beaten down by sin, empowered by grace, redeemed by the One who rides in the desert, we cannot avoid doing business with the world. But the Christ event draws us beyond the marketplace; we are in but not of the world. The Lord is at hand. Have no anxiety about anything. Rejoice in the Lord always. For we have died, and our lives are hid with Christ in God. And what takes place in chronology, what *happens,* is only a matter of life and death in that it most certainly is going to be the death of us whose life is running under the skin and of all the living who have ever lived (it has been the death of them as well). So do we have this treasure in earthen vessels, to show that the transcendent power belongs to God and not to us.

2

Yet God was in Christ reconciling the world to divine purpose, not counting our trespasses against us, and entrusting to us the message of reconciliation. Let us therefore with confidence draw near to the throne of grace, that we may receive mercy and find grace to help in time of need. Creation is brimming with opportunity realized. The time of harvest, the season of rain—each belongs to Yahweh. But even the natural ebb and flow of seasons trembles, sways, in the gathering headwind of God's salvation.

In the world you have tribulation; but be of good cheer, I have overcome the world.

Thank God. Thank God. Because it is not only the world that is overcome but sin, the flesh, and the devil, within the world, and all around, and over and above the world as well. The day is coming when the Earth shall see the headwind of the Lord proceeding from the wilderness, and in that day the Earth shall rise up to an articulation of flowers and of destiny. A moving wall of green-dawning sky, spreading thunder from beyond the sun, slanting and thundering out of the east like smoke rising from a distant fire, the wind of the Lord shall congeal upon myriad creation. Then shall the poor and the afflicted be lifted up and those who have died (disappearing) return with the shouting and clamoring Alleluia-astonishment of beings outside the flesh embodied, flatly jubilant souls, coming from no*where* and shouting down the glory, the purpose, the destiny, and the life of it,

with myriad and glorious faces lifted to the sky, shouting
and praising God in the highest.

Because we are convinced that one has died for all.

And he died for all, that those who live might live no
longer for themselves but for him who for their sake died
and was raised. Therefore we must not be conformed to this
world but rather be transformed by the renewal of our
minds, that we may prove what is the will of God, what is
good and acceptable and perfect. A voice cries: When Israel
was a child I loved him, and out of Egypt I have called my
son. It was I who knew you in the wilderness, in the land
of drought. (The Lord your God is God of gods and Lord of
lords, the great, the mighty, and the terrible God, who is not
partial and takes no bribe.) Yahweh executes justice for the
fatherless and the widows, and loves the sojourners (homeless ones), giving them food and clothing. Love the sojourner
therefore; for you were sojourners in the land of Egypt.

Let us cast off the works of darkness and put on the armor
of light. For Christ took upon himself the curse of hanging,
bore the ignominy of crucifixion, accepted the jeering of
people who had neither ears to hear nor eyes to see. The
Remnant One offered himself not as blood-sacrifice to ap-
pease a wrathful God but as ransom for all sin. Jesus became
the Suffering Servant, the Man of Sorrows who trusted only
Yahweh; it was God-in-Christ who reconciled creation to
Creator. And those who are out of luck, out of work, out of
time: these are they who were freed to embrace life in all its
absurdity, tragedy (without words, necessarily), embracing
sacred and redeemed creation amid all the horror and the

murder and the boasting, with none ever to know how they even can bear it, who are crying so rigid and quiet in the dark night alone. But we can neither make peace with the culture nor find peace outside of it. Eternal life is a quality of existence in this present, this time between the times, God says. And we trying to spend money or just get by, without ever once thinking about how eternal life might be *now,* without ever once thinking that peace on Earth might be hammered out *this year* over against the broken and patchy sunlight of space, thinking: We will know it when it comes; we will know it, all right. And God says: It's already come (whirling along the wind, onward and away, *now,* in this time between times), it's already come.

I am the light of the world; whosoever follows me will not walk in darkness, but will have the light of life.

Then present possibility topples forward, gaining momentum, like someone suddenly descending the stairs from not-yet to now, crashing wildly forward and beyond to the place where Jesus is Lord whether we believe it or not. Yes. Thank God for objective redemption by Wholly Other (going out of sight, getting fainter and fainter the world now); yes, thank God. And this fragmentary, finite hoping against hope is enough; despair is enough, just not apathy: for therein is hopeless nothing exalted, and so does Yahweh come crashing, destroying. Christ Jesus is Lord. And the generations pass away. In these intervening years and with evening lamentation, with weeping, the generations pass away.

The foundations of the world are laid bare and the heavens tell the glory of God. The Holy One will not fail any at last, no matter how wooden or blind, no matter; nor did we choose God (or even life) but rather by Living God were we chosen, and that while we were yet striving with implacable Earth and sin and death. Chosen by Living God transcendent for life over life within living, yes, Jesus, not death.

It will not be death. But those who announce the story must do so in spite of their very real unworthiness and doubt and anxiety. Even so, they confront creation with the Word of grace, digging men and women and children out of the collapsed mine shaft of apathy, breathing life into people who have lost sight of the power and the glory, the greatness of God.

At birth each of us embarks on a path with an unseen goal. No preparation is given, no answers provided. Nor can any escape the earthquake of God: the breaking apart of illusion, the deterioration of the body, the death of those loved. And we are not ready for the great rushing wind of years passing. One day comes adulthood; the next brings thick, complete tiredness. And the experience of Yahweh is all of these— earthquake, rushing wind, life-fatigue. And Yahweh is none of these. Like a long sighing wind of years passing it begins (without knowing, without knowing), and the forlorn homeless child in turn is unaware and more: Did the angels sing for me? Analogy and paradox give way at last to soundless praise (O Lord, thou has searched me and known me!), give way at last to unpredictable and unreasoning tears, the more so that the child has long since grown and gone and died (has what?), the years suddenly disappearing, indistinguishable past and present now, inextricable memories and phantom dreams have been, will be, yes, yes, *are* at last, at last are free (unheeded, joyous), weary and redeemed.

In this is love; not that we loved God but that God loved us.

Yet for a time we have the freedom to drift, to hide, allowing the world to overwhelm us with demonic emptiness. But the truth is that no matter how we may fail or misunderstand or rebel, there is no escape from God-encounter: it is not in our power to commit ourselves everlastingly to hell. No one will be spared the darkness; none will be excluded from the light. In the resurrection of Jesus Christ, Yahweh showed forth full salvation triumphant begun: the ransom is paid; the covenant is with all creation regardless of merit. And though destruction surrounds us like a flood, yet is the Holy One faithful to covenantal bond. The deep diseases of racism, nationalism, and economic imperialism will be overcome. Human divisiveness and exploitation cannot but fall before the Spirit of the Lord. And so shall every tragic contradiction be healed by the One who is All in All, Unsynonymous Other, God. O but it is hard to carry on, to withstand this present evil under which the Earth is groaning, dying, fading in the dead of night; it's hard. And the very Earth itself cries out with all the evil shadows wrapped around and whispering, groaning, cries tomorrow and tomorrow and tomorrow dying inescapable death and shame. But no! The Earth and all therein belong to God: O Lord, our Lord, how glorious is thy name in all the earth!

And now a moment of grace lights up a station platform. A figure dim with dawn steps onto the steaming train and, with an unaccountable sense of freedom, leaves behind old sorrows, old regrets, resentments. But the leaving-behind will not vanish; it will become part of the fabric of daily ongoing reality. Our faith can never soar above historical antecedent. On the contrary, it is revelation that makes the past intelligible.

A small expedition explores deep within the earth, swimming through submerged tunnels, mapping underground chambers, navigating along steep rockfalls. At the end of one day's journey, man-made light is cast for the first time on a steep-sloping white crystalline mass in an immense cavern hundreds of feet high. The foundations of the world are laid bare, and the heavens tell of the glory of God. A voice cries into the echoing darkness: The Lord is my rock, my fortress, and my deliverer, my shield and the hope of salvation, my stronghold.

Perhaps it is more accurate to say that one person lives in ten thousand universes than to insist that ten thousand people live in a single universe. Some of us have brilliant, vivid mental pictures; others have no "mind's eye" whatever. Each individual is utterly unique. And no event or instant can be reproduced, repeated. That is part of the given, the mystery, the way it is. Life courses through each of us, following unique and wonderful dream-rhythms. It begins when we are formed in the womb. And every day thereafter waking unto life, with life running under the skin, running swiftly, irresistibly, to the sea, thinking: I do not know what I am; I do not know. Thinking: In the space between two instants, Mystery shall one day rise up and claim what is no longer of this world (that which never meant anything to begin with, apart from its value to God) but was existing and breathing, being alive, thinking: I do not know what I am; but I believe.

Across the vague shadow of time it whirls now, faster and smoother, gathering as though for some incredible effort to expend, rushing down a sky alive with distant fire, orange and blue approaching-dawn, and on the fading shadows filled with bells (and echoes of the old compulsions overcome), triumphant Living God above the night shines forth in all the living land.

3

It is full time now for you to awake from sleep. For salvation is nearer to us now than when we first believed; the night is far gone; the day is at hand.

And if God is for us, who can be against us?

Who shall separate us from the love of Christ? Shall tribulation, or distress, or persecution, or famine, or nakedness, or peril, or sword? No, in all these things we are more than conquerors through the One who loved us. For I am sure that neither death, nor life, nor angels, nor principalities, nor things present, nor things to come, nor powers, nor height, nor depth, nor anything else in all creation will be able to separate us from the love of God in Christ Jesus our Lord.

The time of decision is now. And the inward passion with which we cling to Unsynonymous Other (without whom our lives are means-less, without meaning), that inward passion is the Spirit of faith-community, holy and living, inseparable from truth, free and transcendent. For all who are led by the Spirit of God are the children of God. And the Spirit bears witness with our spirit that we are children of God, and if children, then heirs, heirs of God and fellow

heirs with Christ, provided we suffer with him in order that
we may also be glorified with him.

Go down, Moses! Go down to Egypt land. For Yahweh has
seen the affliction of the people and knows their sufferings
and has come down to deliver them out of the hand of the
Egyptians. Thank God. Thank God. O I can't have heard
what I know I heard. In the name of God, a miracle beyond
understanding: The voice of the Lord flashes forth in flames
of fire; behold, the cry of the people has come to Yahweh,
who has seen the oppression with which the Egyptians op-
press them. And God says to Moses: Tell this to the people,
"The Lord, the God of your fathers, the God of Abraham,
the God of Isaac, and the God of Jacob, has sent me to you."
And the Lord says to Moses: Go in, tell Pharaoh King of
Egypt to let the people go out of his land. Let the people go,
Pharaoh. Let the people go.

The first and the last: Holyglory rainbows of Incarnate
and Infinite Power, Jesus. Yes, Jesus! The first and the last.
With all heaven reaffirmed and rejoicing now, with all
heaven reaffirming that which we never really thought mat-
tered much anyway, that which was not worth suffering for,
dying for, even living for: the world, the universe, creation,
the faithful and the unfaithful, the loyal and the disloyal,
all. And nevermore to hear about stone-cold apathy, God
says. (Yahweh doesn't want to hear about apathy anymore.)
Live in faith, or in hope, or hope against hope, despair even:
Only no more apathy, God says.

But Yahweh is faithful to the apathetic ones; though we
reject the enabling Word of grace, yet is God faithful.

Behold, the day of the Lord is coming. And on that day there shall be inscribed on the bells of the horses, "Holy to the Lord." Yes, even the horses shall be holy, redeemed, full-arrayed with silver and leather and gold in the clean chill of salvation day. Even the horses. And from his manger bed beholding the suffering of even these, God-in-Christ said: Fashion for them harnesses of silver and leather and gold, and inscribe the bells thereupon with the inscription, "Holy to the Lord," that these my creatures might be lifted up forever, which tonight bear silent witness to my birth into the world of suffering and death.

It is almost over now. Soon it shall be said: Build up, build up, prepare the way, remove every obstruction from my people's way. And also they shall see who never have been told of him, and they shall understand who have never heard of him. While out of that instant the Word surges, heaves against space-time limitation, plunging and rearing and twisting until, at last, dimension-duration gives way under the strain of it—gives way under the wild and terrible thrashing of the Word. Holy to the Lord. Amen.

It is almost over now.

While Mary stands weeping outside the tomb. Holy to the Lord. And the preachers aren't afraid. And the preachers aren't afraid to preach Jesus Christ and him crucified and raised from the dead unto everlasting life. Holy to the Lord. And the prophets aren't afraid. And the children aren't afraid either.

Let the children come to me, and do not hinder them; for to such belongs the kingdom of heaven.

Holy to the Lord. And all the living who have ever lived aren't afraid. Not anymore. Holy to the Lord. Not anymore, they aren't. Not anymore. Amen. Holy to the Lord. Holy to the Lord. Amen.